Crown Hall

Werner Blaser

Mies van der Rohe

Crown Hall

Illinois Institute of Technology, Chicago

The Department of Architecture
Architektur Fakultät

Birkhäuser – Publishers for Architecture
Basel · Boston · Berlin

This publication was supported by:
Diese Publikation wurde gefördert von:
Hans Zwimpfer und seiner Architektengruppe

Translation into English (texts Werner Blaser):
Katja Steiner, Bruce Almberg, Ehingen, Germany and into German (text Pao Chi Chang/Alfred Swenson): Kimi Lum, Vienna, Austria

A CIP catalogue record for this book is available from the Library of Congress, Washington D.C., USA.

Die Deutsche Bibliothek – Cataloging-in-Publication Data

Mies van der Rohe, Crown Hall: Illinois Institute of Technology, The Department of Architecture / Werner Blaser. (Transl. into Engl.: Katja Steiner ...). – Basel ; Boston ; Berlin : Birkhäuser, 2001
ISBN 3-7643-6447-5

This work is subject to copyright. All rights are reserved, whether the whole or part of the material is concerned, specifically the rights of translation, reprinting, re-use of illustrations, recitation, broadcasting, reproduction on microfilms or in other ways, and storage in data banks.
For any kind of use permission of the copyright owner must be obtained.

© 2001 Birkhäuser – Publishers for Architecture, P.O. Box 133, CH-4010 Basel, Switzerland. Member of the BertelsmannSpringer Publishing Group.
© 2001 Werner Blaser, Basel, for all photos and pictorial material. Except:
© 2000 Pao-Chi Chang (Drawing on p. 6/7)

Layout: Werner Blaser, Basel

Litho and typography: Photolitho Sturm AG, Muttenz

Printed on acid-free paper produced of chlorine-free pulp. TCF ∞
Printed in Germany

ISBN 3-7643-6447-5

9 8 7 6 5 4 3 2 1   http://www.birkhauser.ch

Inhaltsverzeichnis		Contents
Crown Hall erleben: Mies und das «Offene». Von Pao-Chi Chang und Alfred Swenson	6–25	Experiencing Crown Hall: Mies and the "Open Region" by Pao-Chi Chang and Alfred Swenson
Crown Hall des IIT in Chicago, 1950–56	26/27	Crown Hall at IIT in Chicago, 1950–56
Die Grundlage	28	The Basis
Zur Situation	29	About the Location
Das Rastermaß	44	The Grid Dimensions
Die Außenhülle	45	The Outer Shell
Die stützenfreie Halle	56	The Hall Without Interior Support
Der Innenraum	57	The Interior
Mies van der Rohe – Chicago-Schule 1938–56	68/69	Mies van der Rohe – Chicago School 1938–56
Mies – Stufen seiner Entwicklung	70/71	Mies – Steps of his Development
Mies persönlich – zur Lehre	72	Mies Personally – About the Teaching
Porträt Mies	74/75	Portrait of Mies
Biographie	76/77	Biography
In kreativer Kraft	80	In Creative Power
Ansprache anläßlich der Einweihungsfeierlichkeiten für die Crown Hall	81	Address at the Dedication of Crown Hall
Nachwort	82	Epilog

Crown Hall, IIT, Ludwig Mies van der Rohe, Chicago, 1950–56. Perspektivische Innenansicht, die die Zone des «Offenen» und die Zone des Alltags zeigt. Personen: IIT-Architekturstudenten und Lehrkörper.
Zeichnung/Collage
von Pao-Chi Chang,
© 2000 Pao-Chi Chang.

Crown Hall, IIT, Ludwig Mies van der Rohe, Chicago, 1950–56. Interior Perspective View showing the Zone of the "Open Region" and the Quotidian Zone. All the figures are IIT architecture students and faculty.
Drawing/Collage
by Pao-Chi Chang,
© 2000 Pao-Chi Chang.

Crown Hall erleben: Mies und das «Offene»

Pao-Chi Chang und Alfred Swenson

Die Crown Hall bedeutete eine einmalige Chance in der Karriere Ludwig Mies van der Rohes. 1938 wurde er zum Direktor der Architekturabteilung des Illinois Institute of Technology (IIT) ernannt, und man ließ ihm freie Hand, einen neuen Lehrplan zu erstellen. 1939 wurde er als Architekt für die Neugestaltung des IIT-Hochschulgeländes ausgewählt und erhielt im Jahr 1950 den Auftrag, ein neues Gebäude für die Architekturabteilung und das Designinstitut zu gestalten. Mies war faktisch sein eigener Bauherr und konnte letztlich ein Gebäude gestalten, das sowohl seine Ideen von Architektur als auch von Architekturunterricht verkörpern würde. Als das Gebäude 1956 fertiggestellt war, bezeichneten es Architekturkritiker wie auch Mies selbst als eine seiner größten Leistungen.

Wir haben beide bei Mies an dieser Hochschule studiert, an der wir später auch selber als Professoren lehren sollten. Mehr als zwei Jahrzehnte unterrichteten wir in diesem Gebäude und erlebten auf diese Weise die herausfordernden und provokativen Qualitäten des von Glaswänden umschlossenen Innenraumes. In diesem außergewöhnlichen Raum hielten wir unsere Lehrveranstaltungen: Pao-Chi Chang leitete die Design-

Experiencing Crown Hall: Mies and the "Open Region"

Pao-Chi Chang and Alfred Swenson

Crown Hall represented a unique opportunity in Ludwig Mies van der Rohe's career. In 1938 he had been appointed Director of the Department of Architecture at Illinois Institute of Technology (IIT) and given a free hand to establish a new curriculum for it. In 1939, he was chosen as the architect for the new IIT Campus, and was commissioned in 1950 to design a new building for the Department of Architecture and the Institute of Design. Mies was in effect his own client, and could at last fulfill the task of designing a building that would embody both his ideas of architecture and architectural education. When the building was completed in 1956, both architectural critics and Mies himself recognized it as one of his major achievements.

We were both students of Mies, and later we would both come to be professors in this school, spending more than two decades of teaching in this building, and experiencing the challenging and provocative qualities of its glass-walled interior. In this great space we taught our courses: Pao-Chi Chang taught fifth-year and graduate design studios, and lectured on theory in architectural design; Alfred Swenson taught second and third-year construction studios and lectured on energy in architecture and building systems. We were in it

a

b

a) Pavillon der deutschen Elektrizitätsindustrie auf der Internationalen Ausstellung Barcelona, Ludwig Mies van der Rohe, 1928–29, 1929 abgetragen. Innenansicht. Berliner Bildbericht, Berlin.

a) German Electrical Industries Pavilion at the Barcelona International Exposition, Ludwig Mies van der Rohe, 1928–29, demolished 1929. Interior view. Berliner Bildbericht, Berlin.

b) Projekt für den deutschen Pavillon auf der Weltausstellung in Brüssel, Ludwig Mies van der Rohe, 1934. Innenperspektive. Bleistift auf Transparentpapier, 26,5 x 43,9 cm. The Mies van der Rohe Archive, The Museum of Modern Art, New York. Schenkung des Architekten. © 2000 The Museum of Modern Art, New York.

b) Project for the German Pavilion for the Brussels World's Fair, Ludwig Mies van der Rohe, 1934. Interior perspective. Pencil on tracing paper, 10" x 17" (26.5 cm x 43.9 cm). The Mies van der Rohe Archive, The Museum of Modern Art, New York. Gift of the architect. © 2000 The Museum of Modern Art, New York.

Übungen für fortgeschrittene und Postgraduate Studenten und las über Theorie des Designs in der Architektur; Alfred Swenson hielt die praktischen Kurse in Entwurfszeichnen für Studierende im zweiten und dritten Jahr und las über Energie in Architektur und Bausystemen. Wir haben dieses Gebäude unter den unterschiedlichsten Bedingungen erlebt – bei Tag und Nacht, zu allen Jahreszeiten, an goldenen Herbstnachmittagen und bei tobenden Schneestürmen im Winter, wenn es im Inneren von Menschen wimmelte oder wenn wir ganz alleine waren. Und so kam es, daß wir allmählich zu unserem ganz persönlichen Verständnis der Crown Hall fanden, welches wir nun in diesem Text erläutern wollen.

Mies konzipierte die Crown Hall scheinbar anders als alle anderen IIT-Bauten. Die Lage des Gebäudes wurde schon in dem von Mies entworfenen Gesamtplan des Hochschulgeländes festgelegt, wobei die vielen kleinen Bauten als «verschiebbare Grundrisse» fungierten, um eine Reihe fließender Räume zu schaffen. Doch die Crown Hall weicht von all den Konventionen, die er für den Campus vorgesehen hatte, ab. Die Grundfläche des Gebäudes ist viel größer als auf dem ursprünglichen Plan; es ist in der Tat das größte Gebäude, das Mies auf dem Hochschulgelände bauen sollte. Die bei früheren Bauten bevorzugten Baumaterialien sind schwarzgestrichene Stahlskelettkonstruktionen, ausgefacht mit gelbem Backstein und durchsichtigem Glas; die Crown Hall weist keine Ziegel auf, nur Stahl und Glas sowie große Flächen Milchglas. Das 6×6-Fuß-Modul, das bei allen anderen Universitätsgebäuden ver-

under all kinds of circumstances, day and night and in all seasons; on golden autumn afternoons and in winter snow storms; when it was crowded with people, and when we were all alone there. It was during this time we gradually came to our understanding of Crown Hall, which we now offer in this essay.

We begin with the observation that Mies seemed to make Crown Hall different from his other IIT campus buildings. The site of the building had already been determined in Mies' campus plan, with its many small buildings treated as "sliding planes" to create a series of flowing spaces. But other than that, Crown Hall departs from all the conventions he had established for the campus. The footprint of the building is much larger than that shown on the original plan, indeed it is the largest Mies would build on the academic campus. The predominant materials of earlier buildings are black-painted steel frames, in-filled with buff brick and clear glass; Crown Hall has no brick, only steel and glass, and large areas of obscure glass as well. The six ft. by six ft. module used in all the other campus buildings is here abandoned for a five ft. by five ft. module. All the other academic buildings are entered directly from the flat plane of the site; Crown Hall's entrance is dramatically raised above grade.

Perhaps Mies made Crown Hall unlike the rest of the campus because he saw in it the chance to realize for the first time a large glass-walled, column-free space – a building type which would become a major theme in his late work. This type was first adumbrated in the German Electrical In-

c) Projekt für eine Konzerthalle, Ludwig Mies van der Rohe, 1942. Collage. Hedrich-Blessing Archive.

c) Project for a Concert Hall, Ludwig Mies van der Rohe, 1942. Collage. Hedrich Blessing Archive.

d) Projekt für ein Drive-in-Restaurant, Ludwig Mies van der Rohe, 1945–48. Foto des Modells. Chicago Historical Society, Hedrich Blessing Archive.

d) Project for a Drive-in Restaurant, Ludwig Mies van der Rohe, 1945–48. Photograph of Model. Chicago Historical Society, Hedrich Blessing Archive.

wendet wurde, wird hier durch ein 5 x 5-Fuß-Modul ersetzt. Die anderen Campusbauten sind direkt ebenerdig zu begehen; der Eingang der Crown Hall wurde in dramatischer Weise über das Geländeniveau erhöht.

Vielleicht konzipierte Mies die Crown Hall deshalb anders, weil er darin seine Chance sah, zum ersten Mal einen großen, von Glaswänden umschlossenen, stützenfreien Raum zu realisieren – einen Gebäudetyp, der in seinem Spätwerk zu einem wichtigen Motiv wurde. Diesen Typ deutete er zum ersten Mal mit dem Pavillon der deutschen Elektrizitätsindustrie auf der Internationalen Ausstellung in Barcelona 1929 an (1928–29, 1929 abgetragen). Der Innenraum dieses kubischen, fensterlosen Baus wurde über eine erhellte Deckenfläche belichtet, und die Wände waren vollständig mit Großfotografien tapeziert, was dem Betrachter die Illusion gab, in einen «virtuellen» Leerraum zu schauen (Abb. a). Die nächste Stufe in dieser Entwicklung zeigte sich 1934 bei dem Projekt für den deutschen Pavillon auf der Weltausstellung in Brüssel, eine große Halle mit einer verglasten Wand, die den Blick auf einen Hof freigab (Abb. b). In seinem Projekt für eine Konzerthalle entwickelte er diese Idee weiter, indem er ein Auditorium konzipierte, das an drei Seiten mit freistehenden Wänden abgegrenzt war, eingeschlossen in einem riesigen, mit verglastem Dach überspannten Industriebauwerk (Abb. c). Dieser Gebäudetyp erreichte seine volle Entfaltung in dem Projekt für ein

dustries Pavilion at the 1929 Barcelona International Exposition (1928–29, demolished 1929). The interior of this cubical windowless building was lighted by a luminous ceiling plane, and the walls were completely covered by photomurals which gave the illusion to the observer of looking into "virtual" space (ill. a). The next development appeared in his project of 1934 for the German Pavilion for the Brussels World's Fair, a large hall with a glazed wall opening to a court (ill. b). The idea emerged further in his Project for a Concert Hall of 1942; here an auditorium defined by free-standing planes was enclosed within a huge glass-roofed industrial structure (ill. c). The type reached full definition in his project of 1945–48 for a Drive-in Restaurant, where a roof plane 152 ft. by 104 ft. was suspended from two steel trusses, spanning in the long direction, sheltering a glass-enclosed space with open dining areas and a central enclosed kitchen (ill. d).

Crown Hall extends the structural steel parti of the Drive-in Restaurant, with an even larger 220 ft. by 120 ft. roof plane, suspended from four 120-ft.-long plate girders six ft. deep, which are supported by columns at the long sides (ill. e). The columns and girders are spaced to form three 60 ft. bays with 20 ft. cantilevers at each end. Under the steel clear span roof, a secondary concrete flat-slab structure, with small bays, rises from the lower level to support the upper level floor. This great glass-enclosed room of the upper level, with

e

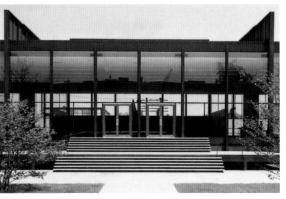

f

e) Crown Hall, IIT, Ludwig Mies van der Rohe, 1950–56. Ansichten.

e) Crown Hall, IIT, Ludwig Mies van der Rohe, 1950–56. Elevations.

f) Crown Hall, IIT, Ludwig Mies van der Rohe, Chicago, 1950–56. Südeingang. Chicago Historical Society, Hedrich Blessing Archive.

f) Crown Hall, IIT, Ludwig Mies van der Rohe, Chicago, 1950–56. South entrance. Chicago Historical Society, Hedrich Blessing Archive.

Drive-in-Restaurant 1945–48. Hier hing von zwei Stahlfachwerkträgern eine etwa 46 x 32 m große Deckenscheibe herab, die, in Längsrichtung gespannt, einen von Glas umschlossenen Raum überdachte, der ineinanderfließende Gasträume und eine zentrale abgeschlossene Küche beherbergte (Abb. d).

Die Crown Hall erweitert die strukturelle Stahlträgergestalt des Drive-in-Restaurants mit einer noch größeren Deckenscheibe, die rund 67 x 37 m misst und die in einer Stahlkonstruktion hängt, welche aus vier rund 37 m langen, 1,8 m hohen Stahlträgern besteht. Diese liegen auf Stützen an den Längsseiten des Gebäudes auf (Abb. e). Die Stützen und Träger sind so angeordnet, daß drei Fassadenfelder von circa 18 m und an den Enden jeweils circa 6 m lange Auskragungen gebildet werden. Das Stahlskelett des frei überspannten Raumes wird von einer trägerlosen Betondeckenstruktur gestützt, die sich aus dem unteren Geschoß nur knapp über die Geländeebene erhebt und an der Außenfassade einen schmalen Flächenraster aufweist. Der große verglaste Raum des oberen Geschosses mit einer Deckenhöhe von 5,5 m war für die Architekturabteilung vorgesehen, wobei alle Unterrichtsstunden in diesem einen offenen Raum stattfinden sollten und alle Studierenden die Arbeiten der anderen sehen können sollten. Die untere Ebene, zum Teil oberirdisch, zum Teil in der Erde versenkt und durch Gadenfenster belichtet, wurde in konventionelle Räume

a ceiling height of eighteen feet, was designed to house the Department of Architecture with all classes meeting in this one open space, where each student could see the work of all the others. The lower level, partly raised above grade and partly recessed, and lighted by clerestory windows, was divided into more conventional rooms to accommodate the Institute of Design. The glass enclosure of the building is supported by steel I-beam mullions spaced ten ft. apart, which run continuously from grade level up through the upper level floor fascia to the roof fascia. The walls are glazed entirely with obscure glass, except for an eleven ft. high ribbon of clear glass that runs around the upper level, and extends to the floor at the entrance bays.

Crown Hall's exterior is a masterpiece of great architecture, exquisitely proportioned and composed. The details are crisp and refined. The overall impression is one of strength and serenity. The steel elements have somehow transcended their mundane origins in the rolling mill and the engineers' calculations. Like a superb work of abstract sculpture, it seems to draw the observers' attention beyond the realm of materiality.

When one approaches the entrance, one encounters the unexpected. The building is entered at the central bays of the upper level on both of the long sides. This, together with the general overall symmetry of the building, suggests that Mies may be following the rules of classical architecture, but

g) Bauakademie, Karl Friedrich Schinkel, Berlin, 1831–35, 1959 abgetragen. Eingang. Institut für Denkmalpflege, Berlin.

g) Bauakademie, Karl Friedrich Schinkel, Berlin, 1831–35, demolished 1959. Entrance. Institut für Denkmalpflege, Berlin.

h) Alumni Memorial Hall, IIT, Ludwig Mies van der Rohe, Chicago, 1945–46. Südansicht. Chicago Historical Society, Hedrich Blessing Archive.

h) Alumni Memorial Hall, IIT, Ludwig Mies van der Rohe, Chicago, 1945–46. South elevation. Chicago Historical Society, Hedrich Blessing Archive.

g

h

eingeteilt und beherbergt das Designinstitut. Die verglasten Flächen der Gebäudehülle sind zwischen I-Träger gespannt, die in circa 3 m großen Abständen stehen und durchgehend vom Geländeniveau über den Rand der Bodenplatte des Hauptgeschosses bis zur Oberkante der Dachplatte führen. Die Außenwände sind rundum mit Milchglas versehen, bis auf ein etwa 3,4 m hohes Bandfenster aus durchsichtigem Glas, das rund um das Hauptgeschoß läuft und in den Eingangsbereichen bis zum Fußboden hinunterreicht.

Das äußere Erscheinungsbild der Crown Hall ist ein Meisterwerk der Baukunst, vorzüglich proportioniert und komponiert. Die Details sind klar und raffiniert. Der Gesamteindruck vermittelt Stärke und Gelassenheit. Die Stahlelemente scheinen ihre irdische Herkunft aus dem Walzwerk und ihre Entstehung in den Bauplänen weit hinter sich gelassen zu haben. Wie ein meisterhaftes Beispiel abstrakter Skulptur vermag Crown Hall, die Aufmerksamkeit des Betrachters über die verdinglichte Welt zu erheben.

Wenn man sich dem Eingang nähert, entdeckt man etwas Unerwartetes. Man kann das Gebäude an beiden Längsseiten im zentralen Bereich des Hauptgeschosses betreten. Dieser Umstand legt zusammen mit der Gesamtsymmetrie des Gebäudes den Gedanken nahe, daß Mies hier die Regeln klassischer Baukunst befolgt habe, aber bald merkt man, daß dies nicht der Fall ist. An dem an der Südseite befindlichen Haupteingang geht man ein paar mit Travertin gepflasterte Stufen hinauf, die in eine rund 18 m breite, ebenfalls mit Travertin belegte Plattform münden. Wenn man sie überquert hat, führen weitere eben solche Stufen zu einer zweiten, kleineren Plattform hinauf. Hier steht man vor zwei Doppeltüren und somit vor der Wahl, durch welche man nun das Gebäude betreten soll (Abb. f). Der erwartete klassische Eingang in der Mittelachse wird unklassisch durch einen I-Träger verstellt. Diese Eingangskonfiguration könnte auf ein anderes, von Mies bewundertes Architekturschulgebäude (1) verweisen, Karl Friedrich Schinkels ebenso unklassische Bauakademie in Berlin (1831–35, 1959 abgetragen), die

soon one finds this is not so. At the principal entrance on the south side, observers ascend a short flight of planar travertine steps to a 60 ft. wide travertine-paved platform. They then cross the platform and climb another flight of similar steps to a smaller platform, where one must choose one of two pairs of doors to enter the building (ill. f). The classically-expected axial entrance is unclassically blocked by a steel mullion. This entrance configuration may be a reference to another school of architecture building admired by Mies (1), Karl Friedrich Schinkel's equally unclassical Bauakademie in Berlin (1831–35, demolished 1959), which also had two entrance doors approached by a flight of steps (ill. g). This deviation from the classical architectural principle of an axial procession (or marche) continues on the interior, where the axis leads to no emphatic central architectural event, as one would find in a classical building (2). Instead observers find themselves in the central exhibition area, defined only by low oak partitions. These partitions were carefully composed by Mies so that a direct view through to the north entrance bay is blocked, but one's gaze is drawn everywhere outward over the tops of the low partitions to the glass walls beyond. The overall effect can be likened to being transposed into a special space – one is presented with a sense of openness of the entire space, with no loss of definition even when one looks back at the south entrance bay.

By contrast, the north entrance is approached by a bridge-like pair of stairs and landing rising to the upper level floor, where one again must choose between two pairs of doors. Here one enters into a narrow vestibule-like space, defined by one low oak partition which extends the full width of the entrance bay. One then walks past this vestibule wall and encounters the great open spaces on either side.

Unlike his precursor clear-span projects for the Concert Hall, where much of the space was interrupted by the walls and ceiling plane of the auditorium, or the Drive-in Restaurant which contained substantial solid elements extending to the

1. Fritz Neumeyer, Mies van der Rohe. Das Kunstlose Wort, Gedanken zur Baukunst, Berlin, 1986, S. 391.

1. Fritz Neumeyer, The Artless Word: Mies van der Rohe on the Building Art, Cambridge, 1991, p. 227.

2. Colin Rowe, «Neo-‹Classicism› and Modern Architecture II», in: The Mathematics of the Ideal Villa and Other Essays, Cambridge, 1976, S. 149.

2. Colin Rowe, "Neo-'Classicism' and Modern Architecture II", in The Mathematics of the Ideal Villa and Other Essays, Cambridge, 1976, p. 149.

ebenfalls zwei über Stufen zu erreichende Eingangstüren aufwies (Abb. g). Diese Abweichung vom klassischen Architekturprinzip einer axial angeordneten Wegführung setzt sich dann im Inneren des Gebäudes fort, denn die Achse führt zu keinem klaren zentralen architektonischen Ereignis, wie man es in einem klassischen Bauwerk erwarten würde (2). Statt dessen befindet sich der Betrachter nun in dem zentralen Ausstellungsbereich, der nur durch niedrige Raumteiler aus Eiche definiert wird. Diese Raumteiler wurden von Mies sorgfältig gestaltet, damit die direkte Sicht bis zum Nordeingangsbereich verstellt wird, der Blick jedoch in alle Richtungen nach außen, über die niedrigen Raumteiler hinweg auf die verglasten Außenwände gelenkt ist. Die Gesamtwirkung kann mit einem Versetzt-Werden an einen außergewöhnlichen Ort verglichen werden – man spürt eine Art Öffnung des ganzen Raums, ohne Definitionsverlust, selbst, wenn man auf den Südeingangsbereich zurückblickt.

Den Nordeingang erreicht man hingegen über eine Art Brücke, die sich aus einem Treppenpaar und einem dazwischenliegenden Plateau bildet und zum Hauptgeschoß führt, auf dem man wieder zwischen zwei Doppeltüren wählen muß. Hier gelangt man in einen schmalen Vorraum, der durch einen niedrigen, sich über die ganze Breite des Eingangsbereichs erstreckenden Eichenraumteiler abgegrenzt wird. Nun geht man um diese Wand herum, und schon treten einem die weitläufigen offenen Räume von beiden Seiten entgegen. Im Gegensatz zu früheren Entwürfen von stützenlos überspannten Räumen wie der Konzerthalle, in der viel Raum durch die Wand- und Deckenscheiben des Auditoriums zunichte gemacht wurde, oder dem Drive-in-Restaurant, in dem einige solide Elemente bis an die Decke reichten, gelang es Mies bei der Crown Hall, das Hauptgeschoß fast vollständig leer zu belassen. Der Raum wird nur durch zwei hohe, schlanke Ent- bzw. Versorgungsschächte und einige niedrige Eichenraumteiler unterbrochen. In diesem außergewöhnlichen Innenraum vergißt man leicht die gewaltige Stahlkonstruktion, die man von draußen gerade noch

ceiling, Mies was able to make the upper level of Crown Hall nearly empty. The space is punctuated only by two small full-height duct shafts and a few low oak partitions. In this remarkable interior, one loses awareness of the great steel structure one has admired on the outside. The beams of the roof plate are hidden by the vast white plane of the acoustic tile ceiling, with its minor rhythmic interruptions of recessed light fixtures and air grills. It is the neutral tranquillity of this planar surface that everywhere deflects the observers' gaze to the empty light-filled space above them. The effect of this ensemble of interior elements is, we believe, exactly what Mies intended: it looks at once simple and natural, yet clearly intentional.

Crown Hall's upper level interior, we believe, is of equal, if not greater significance than the exterior. Here in this vast open space, with this glazed enclosure, we come face to face with Mies' life-long struggle with the philosophical expression of his architecture. Here, we believe, is where his "architecture of truth" is at last clearly realized.

Our attempt to understand the Crown Hall interior began with a reading of Mies' few written statements of his architectural intentions. We found these remarks of 1961 of particular interest, in which he describes his work as a search for truth in architecture:

"In 1900 there was a group of very talented men in Europe who founded the Art Nouveau Movement. They tried to develop everything anew, houses new, dresses new, spoons new, life new, everything new. They thought, however, that it was a question of form. The whole movement didn't last much longer than a typical fashion and nothing came out of it. They were most talented people – there were no finer in the world, and they still could not do it. It then became clear to me that it was not the task of architecture to invent form. I tried to understand what that task was. I asked Peter Behrens, but he could not give me an answer. He did not ask that question. The others said: 'What we build is architecture', but we weren't satisfied with this answer. Maybe they didn't understand the question. We tried to find out. We

bewundert hatte. Die Dachträger sind hinter der riesigen weißen Fläche von schalldämmenden Deckenplatten versteckt, in denen nur kleine rhythmische Unterbrechungen durch versenkte Deckenleuchten und Lüftungsgitter auftreten. Gerade die neutrale Ruhe, die diese glatte Fläche ausstrahlt, ist es, die den Blick der Betrachter, wo immer sie sich befinden, hinauf auf diesen leeren, lichterfüllten Raum lenkt. Die Wirkung dieses Ensembles der Innenelemente ist, unserer Meinung nach, genau das, was Mies angestrebt hat: Es sieht schlicht und natürlich aus, zugleich auch eindeutig absichtsvoll.

Die Innengestaltung des Hauptgeschosses der Crown Hall ist, unserer Ansicht nach, von ebenso großer, wenn nicht noch größerer Bedeutung als die Außenarchitektur. Hier, umgeben von dieser Glashülle in diesem weitläufigen offenen Raum, sind wir hautnah mit dem lebenslangen Ringen Mies van der Rohes um den philosophischen Ausdruck seiner Architektur konfrontiert. Das ist der Ort, an dem seine «Architektur der Wahrheit» endlich klar realisiert wird.

Unser Versuch, den Innenraum der Crown Hall zu verstehen, begann mit der Lektüre der wenigen von Mies verfaßten Äußerungen über seine architektonischen Zielsetzungen. Folgende Bemerkungen aus dem Jahre 1961, die seine Arbeit als eine Suche nach Wahrheit in der Architektur beschreiben, waren für uns von besonderem Interesse:

«Um 1900 hat es eine Gruppe sehr talentierter Männer in Europa gegeben, die die Jugendstil- bzw. ‹Art Nouveau›-Bewegung begründeten. Sie versuchten alles vom Neuen zu entwickeln, Häuser neu, Kleider neu, Löffel neu, das Leben neu, alles neu. Sie dachten jedoch, daß es eine Frage der Form wäre. Die ganze Bewegung hielt sich nicht viel länger als eine Mode für gewöhnlich dauert. Und nichts ist daraus geworden. Es waren alle äußerst talentierte Menschen – es hat auf der Welt keine besseren gegeben, und trotzdem haben sie's nicht geschafft. Es wurde mir damals klar, daß es nicht die Aufgabe der Architektur war, Form zu erfinden. Ich versuchte, ihre wirkliche Aufgabe zu ergründen. Ich fragte Peter Behrens, aber er konnsearched in the quarries of ancient and medieval philosophy. Since we knew it was a question of the truth, we tried to find out what the truth really was. We were very delighted to find a definition of truth by St. Thomas Aquinas: 'Adequatio intellectus et rei', or as a modern philosopher expresses it in the language of today: 'Truth is the significance of fact.' I never forgot this. It was very helpful, and has been a guiding light. To find out what architecture really is took me fifty years – half a century" (3).

Although in this statement Mies gives a definition of truth from Aquinas, it was apparently only a turning point in his search. Having found a satisfactory verbal definition of truth, he says it took him many more years to translate it into an equally satisfying architectural definition of truth. Now Mies also tells us that his interest in philosophy began at the age of about eighteen, when he started to work in the office of the architect Albert Schneider in Aachen circa 1904 (4). There he by chance found in his drawing table a copy of "Die Zukunft" [The Future], a leading intellectual journal of the day; he began reading it regularly and it marked the beginning of his life-long engagement with philosophy and the spiritual aspects of culture. It must have been shortly after this that Mies first posed his question: "What is truth in architecture?", and he tells us that he arrived at his answer some 50 years later, which would be in the early 1950's when Crown Hall was being designed.

We will argue that the remarkable spatial quality which Mies first achieved in the upper level of Crown Hall was an important aspect of his demonstration of architectural truth. All of Mies' other concerns, such as structural clarity, refinement of detail and elegance of proportion help to bring about this demonstration. It was an achievement worthy of the challenging aphorism of Spinoza that Mies alluded to in his "Address at the Dedication of Crown Hall": "All things excellent are as difficult as they are rare" (5).

But how is this building, and especially its spatial qualities, related to Aquinas' definition of truth? His formula, "veritas est adaequatio rei et intellec-

3. Peter Carter, "Mies van der Rohe", Architectural Design, XXXI, 3, March, 1961, S. 97.

3. Peter Carter, "Mies van der Rohe", Architectural Design, XXXI, 3, March, 1961, p. 97.

4. Franz Schulze, Mies van der Rohe. A Critical Biography, Chicago, 1985, S. 17.

4. Franz Schulze, Mies van der Rohe. A Critical Biography, Chicago, 1985, p. 17.

5. Siehe Text S. 81.

5. See text p. 81.

6. Thomas Aquinas, Summa Theologiae, 1266–1273, Prima Pars, Quaestio XVI – «De Veritate», Articulus I: «Quod autem dicitur quod veritas est adaequatio rei et intellectus.»

6. Saint Thomas Aquinas, Summa Theologiae, 1266–1273, Prima Pars, Quaestio XVI – "De Veritate", Articulus I : "Quod autem dicitur quod veritas est adaequatio rei et intellectus".

7. George Steiner, Heidegger, London, 1978.

7. George Steiner, Heidegger, London, 1978.

8. Werner Blaser, Mies van der Rohe: Lehre und Schule, Basel, 1977, S. 284.

8. Werner Blaser, Mies van der Rohe: Principles and School, Basel, 1977, p. 284.

te mir keine Antwort geben. Er stellte diese Frage nicht. Die anderen sagten: ‹Was wir bauen, ist Architektur›, aber wir waren mit dieser Antwort unzufrieden; vielleicht hatten sie die Frage nicht verstanden. Wir suchten weiter. Wir befaßten uns mit der Philosophie des Altertums und des Mittelalters. Da wir wußten, daß es um die Frage der Wahrheit ging, versuchten wir herauszufinden, was Wahrheit eigentlich sei. Befriedigend fanden wir die Definition der Wahrheit bei Thomas von Aquin: ‹Adequatio intellectus et rei›, oder wie ein Philosoph sich in der heutigen Sprache ausdrücken würde: ‹Wahrheit bedeutet Tatsachen›. Ich habe das nie vergessen. Es war sehr hilfreich, so etwas wie eine Leitlinie. Um herauszufinden, was Architektur wirklich ist, brauchte ich 50 Jahre – ein halbes Jahrhundert.» (3)

Obwohl Mies hier eine Definition der Wahrheit nach Thomas von Aquin zitiert, war dies anscheinend nur ein Wendepunkt bei seiner Suche. Nachdem er eine zufriedenstellende verbale Definition der Wahrheit gefunden hatte, benötigte er noch viele Jahre, diese in eine ebenfalls zufriedenstellende architektonische Definition der Wahrheit zu übersetzen. Weiter erfahren wir von Mies, daß er um die 18 Jahre alt war, als er sich für Philosophie zu interessieren begann, zur selben Zeit, als er um 1904 im Architekturbüro von Albert Schneider in Aachen anfing. (4) Dort fand er zufällig in seinem Zeichentisch eine Ausgabe der damals führenden intellektuellen Zeitung «Die Zukunft». Er begann sie regelmäßig zu lesen, und das war der Anfang seiner lebenslangen Beschäftigung mit Philosophie und den geistigen Aspekten der Kultur. Kurz danach dürfte sich Mies zum ersten Mal die Frage gestellt haben: «Was bedeutet Wahrheit in der Architektur?» Und er erzählt uns, daß er erst etwa 50 Jahre später die Antwort darauf fand, also in den frühen fünfziger Jahren, als er gerade dabei war, die Crown Hall zu entwerfen.

Wir behaupten, daß die bemerkenswerte räumliche Qualität, die Mies erstmals mit dem Hauptgeschoß der Crown Hall gelang, ein wichtiger Aspekt seiner Veranschaulichung der architektonischen Wahrheit war. Alle anderen Anliegen von Mies,

tus", "Truth is the correspondence of statement and thing" (6), seems to have no obvious interpretation that would relate to Mies' late architecture, or indeed to any architecture at all. Likewise, the paraphrase by the un-named "modern philosopher", "Truth is the significance of fact", is no more helpful. It is the singular spatial quality of Crown Hall that appeals to the imagination, and yet both these definitions have nothing spatial about them. When asked to explain his work, Mies would offer laconic remarks, always in terms of function or construction, which would indeed be true, but which would give no insight into the spatial character of his buildings. He was certainly not being deceptive, but we believe he left much unsaid.

Our intellectual understanding of Crown Hall began to approach its present form when we were studying at Oxford University some ten years ago. While there, we encountered a book (7) on the work of the German philosopher Martin Heidegger by the American literary critic, George Steiner. When we first opened it, we were struck by the epigraph Steiner had chosen for it; it was the same aphorism of Spinoza alluded to by Mies, only it was given in the original Latin: "Omnia praeclara tam difficilia quam rara sunt." As we read the volume, it became clear that Heidegger as a philosopher had applied himself to the pursuit of truth as intensely as Mies. And indeed we found in our subsequent study of Heidegger's later work, a remarkable intellectual parallel to the work of Mies, a spatial conception of truth that connects Aquinas' "correspondence of statement and thing" to Mies' late work.

How much did Mies know of the work of Heidegger? The only connection we have found is that a copy of Heidegger's "Kant and the Problem of Metaphysics" (the original German edition of 1929) was listed in an inventory of the books in Mies' library when he died. (8) Nevertheless there are some provocative similarities in their lives and work. Mies (1886–1969) and Heidegger (1889–1976) were exact contemporaries, and shared the turbulent German culture of their times. Both had

wie z.B. strukturelle Klarheit, Verfeinerung von Details und Eleganz der Proportionen, tragen dazu bei, diese Veranschaulichung zuwege zu bringen. Es war eine Leistung, die dem provokativen Aphorismus von Spinoza, den Mies bei der Einweihung der Crown Hall zitierte, in nichts nachstand: «Die großen Dinge sind so schwierig, wie sie auch selten sind.» (5)

Aber wie kann dieses Gebäude, und vor allem wie können seine räumlichen Qualitäten mit der von Aquin stammenden Definition der Wahrheit in Zusammenhang gebracht werden? Seine Formel, «veritas est adaequatio rei et intellectus», «Wahrheit ist die Gleichheit von Aussage und Ding», (6) scheint keine klare Interpretation aufzuweisen, die mit Mies van der Rohes später Architektur, oder mit irgendeiner Architektur überhaupt zu tun haben könnte. Und die Paraphrase auf den nicht genannten «modernen Philosophen», «Wahrheit bedeutet Tatsachen», hilft uns auch nicht weiter. Die einzigartige räumliche Qualität der Crown Hall ist es, die so reizvoll auf unsere Vorstellungskraft wirkt, aber keine der beiden Definitionen haben etwas Räumliches an sich. Immer wenn Mies aufgefordert wurde, seine Werke zu erläutern, antwortete er mit lakonischen Bemerkungen, immer in bezug auf Funktion oder Konstruktion, Antworten, die tatsächlich stimmten, aber die keinerlei Einsicht in den räumlichen Charakter seiner Bauten verschafften. Er wollte keineswegs irreführen, aber wir sind der Ansicht, daß er vieles verschwiegen hat.

Unser intellektuelles Verständnis der Crown Hall begann seine gegenwärtige Form anzunehmen, als wir vor rund zehn Jahren an der Oxford University forschten. Wir entdeckten damals ein Buch des amerikanischen Literaturkritikers George Steiner über das Werk des deutschen Philosophen Martin Heidegger. (7) Als wir es das erste Mal aufschlugen, fiel uns sofort das von Steiner ausgewählte Epigraph ins Auge. Es handelte sich um denselben Aphorismus von Spinoza, auf den Mies hingewiesen hat, nur war er hier auf Lateinisch abgedruckt: «Omnia praeclara tam difficilia quam rara sunt.» Als wir das Werk lasen, wurde uns klar,

a strict Roman Catholic upbringing, Mies in Aachen as the son of a stonemason, and Heidegger at Messkirch in Baden-Wurttemberg as the son of a church sexton – but both would later abandon the formal practice of their faith. Both had intellectual masters or mentors who helped to establish them in their respective fields, with whom they would later break. Mies' master was the architect Peter Behrens (1868–1940) for whom he worked in Berlin during 1908–1912 and Heidegger's was the philosopher Edmund Husserl (1859–1938) under whom he served as an assistant teacher at the University of Freiburg during 1918–1922. Both rose to prominence in the feverish years of the Weimar Republic; Mies with the building of the Weissenhof Siedlung in Stuttgart (1927) and the Barcelona Pavilion (1929), and Heidegger with the publication of "Being and Time" (1927) and "Kant and the Problem of Metaphysics" (1929). Both had encounters with the Nazis; Mies with the closing of the Bauhaus and the design of the Brussels Pavilion, and Heidegger during his short tenure as Rector of the University of Freiburg. They then both went into exile. Mies left Germany for Chicago in 1938, and Heidegger withdrew into a kind of internal exile for the rest of the Nazi period and the subsequent Allied occupation. Finally, after the age of 70, both would make symbolic visits to Greece. It was in this later period of exile that both intensified their search for truth, and the parallels in their work emerge.

This parallel construction begins with Heidegger's essay "On the Essence of Truth", first delivered as a lecture in 1932, published in German in 1943 and first translated into English in 1949. Heidegger begins his discussion with the same definition of truth from Aquinas quoted by Mies: "Veritas est adaequatio rei et intellectus". He goes on to point out that this notion of "correspondence of statement and thing" contains an inherent conflict: "How is the statement able to correspond to something else, the thing, precisely by persisting in its own essence?"(9) He then sets forth his resolution of this conflict with his remarkable concept of "das Offene" or the "open region":

9. Martin Heidegger, «Vom Wesen der Wahrheit», in: Wegmarken, Frankfurt am Main, 1967. S. 183. © 1969, Vittorio Klostermann Verlag.

9. David Farrell Krell, Editor, Martin Heidegger: Basic Writings, New York, 1977, "On the Essence of Truth", p. 123.
English translations © 1977 by Harper & Row Publishers, Inc., reprinted by permission of HarperCollins Publishers, Inc.

daß sich Heidegger als Philosoph ebenso intensiv auf die Suche nach der Wahrheit begeben hatte wie Mies. Und in der Tat entdeckten wir bei unserem darauf folgenden Studium der späten Werke Heideggers eine bemerkenswerte gedankliche Parallele zu dem Werk Mies van der Rohes, eine räumliche Konzeption der Wahrheit, die Aquins «Gleichheit von Aussage und Ding» mit dem späten Werk Mies van der Rohes verbindet.

Wie sehr war Mies mit dem Werk Heideggers vertraut? Die einzige uns bekannte Verbindung besteht in einer Ausgabe von Heideggers «Kant und das Problem der Metaphysik» (1929), die in der Bibliotheksliste im Nachlaß Mies van der Rohes angeführt wurde. (8) Nichtsdestoweniger bestehen markante Ähnlichkeiten in ihrem Leben und ihrem Werk. Mies (1886–1969) und Heidegger (1889–1976) waren Zeitgenossen, und beide erlebten die turbulente deutsche Kultur dieser Zeit. Beide waren streng katholisch erzogen worden; Mies in Aachen als Sohn eines Steinmetz und Heidegger in Meßkirch in Baden-Württemberg als Sohn eines Mesners – aber beide sollten später aus der Kirche austreten. Beide hatten intellektuelle Meister oder Mentoren, mit deren Hilfe sie sich auf ihrem jeweiligen Gebiet etablieren konnten und mit denen sie später brechen sollten. Mies van der Rohes Lehrer war der Architekt Peter Behrens (1868–1940), für den er 1908–1912 in Berlin arbeitete, und Heideggers Lehrer war der Philosoph Edmund Husserl (1859–1938), unter dem er 1918–1922 als Assistent an der Universität Freiburg lehrte. Beide hatten ihre ersten Erfolge während der aufregenden Jahren der Weimarer Republik; Mies mit der Errichtung der Weißenhofsiedlung in Stuttgart (1927) und des Barcelona-Pavillons (1929) und Heidegger mit der Veröffentlichung seiner Werke «Sein und Zeit» (1927) und «Kant und das Problem der Metaphysik» (1929). Beide kamen mit dem Nationalsozialismus in Berührung; Mies durch die Schließung des Bauhauses und die Gestaltung des Brüssel-Pavillons und Heidegger während seiner Zeit als Rektor der Universität Freiburg. Danach gingen beide in die Emigration. Mies verließ Deutschland und wanderte 1938 nach Chicago

"What is stated by the presentative statement is said of the presented thing in just such a manner as that thing, as presented, is. The 'such as' has to do with the presenting and its presented. Disregarding all 'psychological' preconceptions, as well as those of any 'theory of consciousness', to present here means to let the thing stand opposed as object. As thus placed, what stands opposed must traverse *an open field of opposedness* and nevertheless must maintain its stand as a thing and show itself as something withstanding. This appearing of the thing in traversing a field of opposedness takes place within an *open region,* the openness of which is not first created by the presenting but rather is only entered into and taken over as a *domain of relatedness* ... All working and achieving, all action and calculation, keep within an *open region* within which beings, with regard to what they are and how they are, can properly take their stand and become capable of being said." [Our italics] (10)

Heidegger then goes on to identify truth and the "open region" with the Greek word aletheia (αληθεια), which is usually translated as "truth", but which he turns as "unconcealment":

"Western thinking in its beginning conceived this open region as ta aletheia, the unconcealed. If we translate aletheia as 'unconcealment' rather than 'truth', this translation is not merely more literal; it contains the directive to rethink the ordinary concept of truth in the sense of the correctness of statements and to think it back to that still uncomprehended disclosedness and disclosure of beings." (11)

Clearly Heidegger is dissatisfied with much of the classical development of Western metaphysics, and wishes to withdraw from Cartesian subjectivism to the simpler and more profound insights of the pre-Socratics. In the "Letter on 'Humanism'" (1947), Heidegger traces the origin of the "open region" to Heraclitus:

"The saying of Heraclitus (Fragment 119) goes: 'Ethos anthropoi daimon'. This is usually translated, 'A man's character is his daimon.' This translation thinks in a modern way, not a Greek one.

10. Heidegger, «Vom Wesen der Wahrheit», in: ders.: Wegmarken, S. 184.

10. Krell, Heidegger, "On the Essence of Truth", pp. 123–124.

11. Heidegger, «Vom Wesen der Wahrheit», S. 188.

11. Krell, Heidegger, "On the Essence of Truth", pp. 127–128.

aus, und Heidegger trat eine Art innere Emigration an, die während der restlichen Naziherrschaft und der darauffolgenden Besatzung der alliierten Mächte andauerte. Schließlich, als sie schon über 70 waren, begaben sich beide auf eine symbolische Reise nach Griechenland. Es war während dieser späten Periode des Exils, daß sie ihre Suche nach Wahrheit intensivierten und die Parallelen in ihren Werken klar zu Tage traten.

Diese parallele Entwicklung beginnt mit Heideggers Schrift «Vom Wesen der Wahrheit», die ursprünglich als Vortrag 1932 gehalten, 1943 in Deutsch veröffentlicht und zum ersten Mal 1949 ins Englische übersetzt wurde. Heidegger beginnt seine Abhandlung mit derselben Definition der Wahrheit von Aquin, die bei Mies zitiert wird: «Veritas est adaequatio rei et intellectus.» In der Folge weist er darauf hin, daß diese Idee der «Gleichheit von Aussage und Ding» einen inhärenten Widerspruch in sich trägt: «Wie vermag die Aussage gerade durch ein Beharren auf ihrem Wesen einem Anderen, dem Ding, sich anzugleichen?» (9) Dann legt er mit seiner außergewöhnlichen Vorstellung des «Offenen» oder des «offenen Bezirks» seine Aufhebung dieses Widerspruches dar:

«Die vorstellende Aussage sagt ihr Gesagtes so vom vorgestellten Ding, wie es als dieses ist. Das ‹So–Wie› betrifft das Vor-stellen und sein Vor-gestelltes. Vor-stellen bedeutet hier, unter Ausschaltung aller ‹psychologischen› und ‹bewußtseinstheoretischen› Vormeinungen, das Entgegenstehenlassen des Dinges als Gegenstand. Das Entgegenstehende muß als das so Gestellte ein *offenes Entgegen* durchmessen und dabei doch in sich als das Ding stehenbleiben und als ein Ständiges sich zeigen. Dieses Erscheinen des Dinges im Durchmessen eines Entgegen vollzieht sich innerhalb eines *Offenen,* dessen Offenheit vom Vorstellen nicht erst geschaffen, sondern je nur als ein *Bezugsbereich* bezogen und übernommen wird... Jedes Werken und Verrichten, alles Handeln und Berechnen hält sich und steht im *Offenen eines Bezirks,* innerhalb dessen das Seiende als das, was es ist und wie es ist, sich eigens stellen und sagbar werden kann.» [Unsere Hervorhebungen] (10)

Ethos means abode, dwelling place. The word names the open region in which man dwells ... The fragment says: Man dwells, insofar as he is man, in the nearness of god ... [or] 'The (familiar) abode is for man the open region for the presencing of god (the unfamiliar one).'" (12)

Finally, in "The End of Philosophy and the Task of Thinking" (1966), Heidegger goes on to identify the "open region" with an even more primitive image, the "Lichtung" (literally "lighting") or "forest clearing", a familiar sight to him ever since his youth at Messkirch in the Black Forest:

"To open something means to make it light, free and open, e. g., to make the forest free of trees at one place. The free space thus originating is the clearing ... Light can stream into the clearing, into its openness, and let brightness play with darkness in it. But light never first creates openness. Rather, light presupposes openness. However, the clearing, the open region, is not only free for brightness and darkness but also for resonance and echo, for sound and the diminishing of sound. The clearing is the open region for everything that becomes present and absent." (13)

Now it is certainly possible that Mies may have read these works of Heidegger, either in German or in English translation, although we can find no direct evidence that he did. But the parallel lines of their thought seem unmistakable. Heidegger's exposition of truth consisted of two facets, "aletheia" and "das Offene", the physical and the metaphysical. In Mies' search for truth, these two facets were first developed independently in his later work in Chicago, and finally coalesce in his design for Crown Hall.

Thus while Heidegger first sets forth his concept of truth as the "open region", this abstract space to achieve the correspondence of statement and thing, in "The Essence of Truth" in 1932, Mies had first suggested his architectural "open region" in the German Electrical Industries Pavilion of 1929. And Heidegger's other facet of truth, the pre-classical notion of aletheia or "unconcealment" can be identified with Mies' advocacy of the equally unadorned, and craftsmanlike use of traditional

12. Heidegger, «Brief über den ‹Humanismus›», in: ders.: Wegmarken, a.a.O., S. 354–55.

12. Krell, Heidegger , "Letter on 'Humanism' ", pp. 233–234.

13. Martin Heidegger, Zur Sache des Denkens, Tübingen, 1969, «Das Ende der Philosophie und die Aufgabe des Denkens», S. 72.

13. Krell, Heidegger , "The End of Philosophy and the Task of Thinking", p. 384.

14. Ludwig Mies van der Rohe, Deutsches Originalmanuskript, 1938. Library of Congress, Washington, D. C.

14. Philip Johnson, Mies van der Rohe, New York, 1947, pp. 191–195. Reprinted by permission, © 1947 The Museum of Modern Art.

Nun setzt Heidegger die Wahrheit und das Offene mit dem griechischen Wort aletheia (αληθεια) gleich, das normalerweise mit «Wahrheit» übersetzt wird, das er aber hier als «Unverborgenheit» auslegt:
«Dieses Offene hat das abendländische Denken in seinem Anfang begriffen als ta aletheia, das Unverborgene. Wenn wir aletheia statt mit ‹Wahrheit› durch ‹Unverborgenheit› übersetzen, dann ist diese Übersetzung nicht nur ‹wörtlicher›, sondern sie enthält die Weisung, den gewohnten Begriff der Wahrheit im Sinne der Richtigkeit der Aussage um- und zurückzudenken in jenes noch Unbegriffene der Entborgenheit und der Entbergung des Seienden.» (11)
Es ist offensichtlich, daß Heidegger mit der Entwicklung der klassischen abendländischen Metaphysik nicht zufrieden ist und daß er sich vom cartesischen Subjektivismus zurückziehen und sich den einfacheren und tiefschürfenderen Erkenntnissen der vorsokratischen Denker widmen möchte. In seinem «Brief über den ‹Humanismus›» (1947) führt er den Ursprung des «Offenen» auf Heraklit zurück:
«Der Spruch des Heraklit lautet (Frgm. 119): Ethos anthropoi daimon. Man pflegt allgemein zu übersetzen: ‹Seine Eigenart ist dem Menschen sein Dämon.› Diese Übersetzung denkt modern, aber nicht griechisch. Ethos bedeutet Aufenthalt, Ort des Wohnens. Das Wort nennt den offenen Bezirk, worin der Mensch wohnt ... Der Spruch sagt, der Mensch wohnt, insofern er Mensch ist, in der Nähe Gottes. [Oder] ‹Der (geheure) Aufenthalt ist dem Menschen das Offene für die Anwesung des Gottes (des Un-geheuren).›» (12)
Zum Schluß assoziiert Heidegger in «Das Ende der Philosophie und die Aufgabe des Denkens» (1966) das «Offene» mit einem noch primitiveren Bild, der «Lichtung», ein für ihn seit der Kindheit in Meßkirch im Schwarzwald vertrauter Anblick.
«Etwas lichten bedeutet: etwas leicht, etwas frei und offen machen, z.B. den Wald an einer Stelle frei machen von Bäumen. Das so entstehende Freie ist die Lichtung ... Das Licht kann nämlich in die Lichtung, in ihr Offenes, einfallen und in ihr die

architectural materials such as timber, stone and brick, which he announced in his "Inaugural Address as Director of the Department of Architecture at IIT" in 1938:
"... Let us guide our students over the road of discipline from materials, through function, to creative work. Let us lead them into the healthy world of primitive building methods, where there was meaning in every stroke of an axe, expression in every bite of a chisel. Where can we find greater structural clarity than in the wooden buildings of old? Where else can we find such unity of material, construction and form? ... What better examples could there be for young architects? Where else could they learn such simple and true crafts than from these unknown masters? ... Nothing can express the aim and meaning of our work better than the profound words of St. Augustine: 'Beauty is the splendor of Truth.'" (14)
Was Mies not "thinking back" architecture to its primitive roots, to "that still uncomprehended disclosedness and disclosure of beings" that Heidegger too was seeking?
In 1942, Mies again took up the exploration of his "open region" with his project for a Concert Hall; the collage was a vivid statement of a great clear-span space defined by natural light from the skylights above. And during 1945–48, he continued his development of this theme with the project for the Drive-in Restaurant, with its suspended roof plate and all-glass walls, pointing towards the far more sophisticated "open region" of the Crown Hall interior. Both projects were never realized, but Mies separated their formal qualities from their intended functions, and took them as preparatory sketches for further development.
In 1945–46, Mies built his first academic building on the IIT Campus, Alumni Memorial Hall. It was his first thoroughgoing demonstration of the "unconcealed" and craftsmanlike use of unpretentious materials – steel, glass, brick and oak – his statement of aletheia. Built at the same time that Heidegger is writing his "Letter on 'Humanism'" (published 1947) with its pre-Socratic invocations, it also marked Mies' first use of unclassical,

Helle mit dem Dunkel spielen lassen. Aber niemals schafft das Licht erst die Lichtung, sondern jenes, das Licht, setzt diese, die Lichtung, voraus. Indes ist die Lichtung, das Offene, nicht nur frei für Helle und Dunkel, sondern auch für den Hall und das Verhallen, für das Tönen und das Verklingen. Die Lichtung ist das Offene für alles An- und Abwesende.» (13)

Es ist sicherlich möglich, daß Mies diese Werke von Heidegger gelesen hat, entweder auf deutsch oder in der englischen Übersetzung, obwohl wir keinen direkten Hinweis dafür finden konnten. Aber die Parallelen, die die Gedankengänge der beiden aufweisen, scheinen unübersehbar zu sein. Heideggers Darstellung der Wahrheit bestand in zwei Aspekten, in aletheia und dem «Offenen», dem Physischen und dem Metaphysischen. Auf seiner Suche nach Wahrheit entwickelte Mies in seinem Spätwerk in Chicago diese beiden Aspekte zuerst unabhängig voneinander weiter, um sie dann schließlich in der Crown Hall zu vereinen.

Während Heidegger also erst 1932 in «Vom Wesen der Wahrheit» sein Konzept der Wahrheit als das «Offene» darlegt, diesen abstrakten Raum, um die Gleichheit von Aussage und Ding zu erreichen, hat Mies das «Offene» schon 1929 in seinem Pavillon der deutschen Elektrizitätsindustrie architektonisch zur Sprache gebracht. Und Heideggers zweiter Aspekt der Wahrheit, die vorklassische Idee der aletheia oder der «Unverborgenheit», kann mit der Miesschen Verfechtung der in gleicher Weise schlichten und sich auf das Handwerk stützenden Verwendung von traditionellen Baumaterialien, wie Holz, Stein und Ziegel, assoziiert werden, wie er sie 1938 in seiner Antrittsrede als Direktor der Architekturabteilung am IIT ausführte:

«...Deshalb führen wir unsere Studenten den zuchtvollen Weg vom Material über die Zwecke der Gestaltung. Wir wollen sie in die gesunde Welt primitiver Bauten führen, dort, wo noch jeder Beilhieb etwas bedeutet und wo ein Meißelschlag eine wirkliche Aussage war. Wo tritt mit gleicher Klarheit das Gefüge eines Hauses oder Baus mehr hervor als in den Holzbauten der Alten? Wo mehr

or pre-classical symmetry – there were two equal, but widely spaced entrances (II. h). This same configuration appears in pre-classical Greek architecture, for example in the Temple of Hera I (sixth century BC) at Paestum (II. i), which also has two doors, and a central column on the entrance front. Mies would follow this pre-classical symmetry, with no pathway on the central axis leading to a major architectural event, in nearly all of his subsequent buildings including Crown Hall. Indeed, his placement of the steel mullion on the axis of Crown Hall has a pre-classical Greek counterpart in the little Temple A (seventh century BC) at Prinias on Crete (II. k), where the central column of the entrance portico squarely blocks the door.

Confronting the exterior of Crown Hall, free-standing like a Greek temple, with the calm elegance of its clear structure, one thinks of a line of poetry by Parmenides, another pre-Socratic philosopher quoted by Heidegger (15):

"Emen aletheies eukukleos atremes etor".

"The untrembling heart of well-rounded unconcealment".

Do not Parmenidies' words describe the compelling presence of this naked steel frame, so carefully refined by Mies?

Mies disclosed the structure on the exterior of Crown Hall, with its upward-projecting plate girders and its outward-projecting columns and mullions, "un-concealed" in the spirit of Heidegger's aletheia. He then deliberately set aside this "un-

15. Heidegger, «Das Ende der Philosophie und die Aufgabe des Denkens», in: Zur Sache des Denkens, S. 74.

15. Krell, Heidegger, "The End of Philosophy and the Task of Thinking", p. 387.

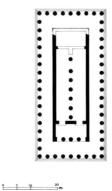

i) Heratempel I, Paestum, 6. Jh. v. Chr. Grundriß.

i) Temple of Hera I, Paestum, sixth century BC. Plan.

die Einheit von Material, Konstruktion und Form? ... Wo anders sollten junge Architekten aufwachsen als in der frischen Luft dieser gesunden Welt, und wo anders sollten sie einfach und klug handeln lernen als bei diesen unbekannten Meistern? ... Durch nichts wird Ziel und Sinn unserer Arbeit mehr erschlossen als durch das tiefe Wort von St. Augustin: ‹Das Schöne ist der Glanz des Wahren!›» (14)

War das nicht von Mies ein «Zurückdenken» der Architektur zu ihren primitiven Wurzeln, zu «jenem noch Unbegriffenen der Entborgenheit und der Entbergung des Seienden», nach dem sich auch Heidegger auf der Suche befand?

1942 nahm Mies seine Erforschung des «Offenen» mit seinem Projekt für eine Konzerthalle wieder auf; die Collage war eine lebendige Darstellung eines großen, frei überspannten Raums, der durch natürliches Licht aus den Oberlichten definiert wurde. Und 1945–48 entwickelte er dieses Thema im Projekt für das Drive-in-Restaurant mit der hängenden Deckenscheibe und den vollständig verglasten Wänden weiter, hin zu dem überaus raffinierten «Offenen» des Innenraums, den wir in der Crown Hall vorfinden. Keines dieser beiden Projekte wurde realisiert, aber Mies trennte ihre formalen Qualitäten von ihren intendierten Funktionen und betrachtete sie als Vorarbeiten für künftige Bauten.

1945–46 baute Mies sein erstes Universitätsgebäude auf dem IIT-Gelände, die Alumni Memorial

concealment" within the building, suppressing the structure to create the metaphysical presence of its interior, an apparition of Heidegger's "open region". The white plane of the ceiling and the gray terrazzo floor plane define the great light-flooded space; the only other elements within it are the two duct-shafts, the low partitions, and the transient sea of student drawing tables spread over the floor. At the enclosing glass walls, the translucent band of glass limits the exterior view of human activities at ground level; this band, together with the low partitions, defines a "quotidian" zone in which the familiar everyday activities of teaching and learning occur. Above the imaginary plane at the tops of the low partitions and translucent glass band is an inaccessible and outreaching zone of space for the free play of light and imagination. One's vision is drawn to this "open region" flowing out in all directions through the upper band of clear glass windows towards the surrounding trees and sky at all times of the day and night (see ill. p. 6/7).

In our time in Crown Hall, we had often looked up at this upper zone, for visual relief, for reflection, even for inspiration, but only after many years did we at last identify it with Heidegger's "open region", this space where statement can correspond with thing, this "field of opposedness", this "domain of relatedness". Heidegger said it was the abstract site of "... All working and achieving, all action and calculation", where "... beings, with regard to what they are and how they are, can properly take their stand and become capable of being said." Mies made his demonstration of "aletheia" on the exterior of Crown Hall, but on the interior he created this empty, nearly abstract upper zone not only to give the students daylight, but as a part of his architectural education program, to invite them to find their own interpretation of truth in architecture.

We also recognized in this space a convergence of philosophical and architectural images. Are not the opaque roof and luminous walls of Mies' Crown Hall interior a provocative inversion of Heidegger's "Lichtung" or "forest clearing", with its

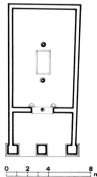

k) Tempel A, Prinias, Kreta, 7. Jh. v. Chr. Grundriß.

k) Temple A, Prinias, Crete, seventh century BC. Plan.

Hall. Es war seine erste konsequente Demonstration der «unverborgenen» und somit sich auf das Handwerk stützenden Verwendung einfacher Materialien – Stahl, Glas, Backstein und Eiche: seine Darstellung der aletheia. Mit diesem Bauwerk, das zur selben Zeit errichtet wurde, als Heidegger seinen «Brief über den ‹Humanismus›» seiner Beschwörung vorsokratischer Vorstellungen schrieb (1947 veröffentlicht), wandte Mies zum ersten Mal die unklassische oder vorklassische Symmetrie an – er baute zwei gleiche, aber weit auseinanderliegende Eingänge (Abb. h). Diese Konfiguration kommt in der vorklassischen griechischen Architektur vor, z.B. beim Heratempel I (6. Jh. v. Chr.) in Paestum (Abb. i), der auch zwei Türen und eine zentrale Säule an der Eingangsfassade aufweist. Diese vorklassische Symmetrie, ohne Wegführung an der Mittelachse zu einem klaren zentralen architektonischen Ereignis, verfolgt Mies von nun an bei fast allen späteren Bauten einschließlich der Crown Hall. Seine Plazierung dieses I-Trägers an der Mittelachse der Crown Hall hat in der Tat ihr Gegenstück in dem kleinen Tempel A (7. Jh. v. Chr.) bei Prinias auf Kreta (Abb. k), dessen zentrale Säule des Eingangsportikus genau in der Mitte steht und den Weg blockiert.

Ist man mit dem äußeren Erscheinungsbild der Crown Hall konfrontiert – wie ein griechischer Tempel freistehend, mit der ruhigen Eleganz seiner klaren Struktur –, denkt man an eine Zeile aus einem Gedicht von Parmenides, einem weiteren bei Heidegger zitierten vorsokratischen Philosophen (15):

«Emen aletheies eukukleos atremes etor», «der Unverborgenheit, der gutgerundeten, nichtzitterndes Herz».

Beschreiben die Worte des Parmenides nicht jene unwiderstehliche Präsenz des nackten, von Mies so sorgfältig verfeinerten Stahlskeletts?

Mies entbarg die Struktur der Crown Hall auf der Außenseite, mit ihren hochragenden Blechträgern und ihren vorspringenden Stützen und I-Trägern, «unverborgen» im Geiste der Heideggerschen aletheia. Dann legte er im Inneren des Gebäudes diese «Unverborgenheit» absichtlich ab; durch Auf-

dark walls of trees and luminous sky above? In this space do we not glimpse that tenuous realm of "the open region for everything that becomes present and absent"?

Finally, we can see Crown Hall as an embodiment of the dichotomy of world and word, of the physical and metaphysical. On the exterior Mies used the physical qualities of steel and glass to create a presence of abstract monumentality. With the interior, he created what we have come to call a space of intellection – the "open region" – as its subtle climactic event, an almost direct manifestation of the philosopher's word.

Pao-Chi Chang studied architecture at St. John's University, Shanghai and at Illinois Institute of Technology, where Mies van der Rohe was her adviser for her master's degree thesis project, the Chicago Convention Hall. After working in Mies's office, she went to the Chicago Office of Skidmore, Owings & Merrill where she served as Senior Architectural Designer and Project Architectural Designer for many building types ranging from 17 Dan Ryan/Kennedy Line Rapid Transit Stations in Chicago to the Sears Tower. She then founded the firm of Alfred Swenson Pao-Chi Chang Architects where she is a partner. She taught as a professor of architecture at Illinois Institute of Technology for over 20 years, and as a visiting studio professor at Harvard Graduate School of Design. She has lectured and published extensively in the fields of architecture and architectural criticism.

Alfred Swenson studied architecture at Illinois Institute of Technology, receiving bachelor's and master's degrees. He served as an Architectural Designer at C.F. Murphy Associates for the Richard J. Daley Center Courthouse and Office Building. He then founded the firm of Alfred Swenson Pao-Chi Chang Architects where he is a partner. He taught as a professor of architecture at Illinois Institute of Technology for over 25 years,

hebung der Struktur schuf er die metaphysische Präsenz des Innenraumes, eine Versinnbildlichung des Heideggerschen «Offenen». Die weiße Deckenscheibe und die graue terrazzoverkleidete Bodenscheibe begrenzen den großen, hell beleuchteten Raum; die einzigen sonstigen Elemente sind zwei Ent- bzw. Versorgungsschächte, die niedrigen Raumteiler und die flüchtig über den Raum verstreuten Zeichentische der Studierenden. Das als Raumhülle umspannende Milchglasband schränkt den Blick nach außen und auf die Menschen auf Geländeebene ein; dieses Band definiert zusammen mit den niedrigen Raumteilern eine Zone des «Alltags», in der die gewohnten täglichen Aktivitäten des Lehrens und Lernens stattfinden. Oberhalb der imaginären Ebene, die mit den oberen Kanten der Raumteiler bzw. dem Rand des Milchglasbandes aufhört, ist eine unerreichbare und nach außen greifende Zone, ein Bereich für das freie Spiel von Licht und Phantasie. Der Blick wird auf dieses «Offene» gelenkt und fließt durch das obere Bandfenster aus durchsichtigem Glas hinaus, in alle Richtungen, zu den Bäumen und dem Himmel, bei Tag und Nacht (s. Abb. S. 6/7).

Während unserer Zeit in der Crown Hall hatten wir oft zu dieser oberen Zone geblickt, visuelle Erleichterung, Reflexion, sogar Inspiration suchend, aber erst nach vielen Jahren assoziierten wir sie mit Heideggers «Offenem», jenem Raum, in dem die Gleichheit von Aussage und Ding möglich ist, jenem «Entgegen», jenem «Bezugsbereich». Heidegger nannte es den abstrakten Ort «jedes Werkens und Verrichtens, alles Handelns und Berechnens», wo «... das Seiende als das, was es ist und wie es ist, sich eigens stellen und sagbar werden kann». Mies vollbrachte seine Darstellung der aletheia am Äußeren der Crown Hall, aber im Inneren schuf er diese leere, fast abstrakte obere Zone nicht nur, um den Studierenden Tageslicht zu geben, sondern als Teil seiner Architekturlehre, um sie einzuladen, ihre eigene Interpretation von Wahrheit in der Architektur zu finden.

Darüber hinaus erkannten wir in diesem Raum eine Konvergenz philosophischer und architekto-

and as a visiting studio professor at Harvard Graduate School of Design. He has lectured and published extensively in the fields of architecture and architectural criticism.

nischer Vorstellungen. Sind nicht das undurchsichtige Dach und die erhellten Wände des Innenraums von Mies van der Rohes Crown Hall eine provokante Umkehrung der «Lichtung» Heideggers, mit ihren dunklen Wänden aus Bäumen und dem hellen Himmelsgewölbe? Erhaschen wir nicht in diesem Raum jenen Hauch eines Reichs des «Offenen für alles An- und Abwesende»?
Endlich können wir die Crown Hall als Verkörperung der Dichotomie der Welt und des Wortes, des Physischen und Metaphysischen begreifen. Für die Außenseite verwendete Mies die physischen Qualitäten des Stahls und des Glases, um eine Präsenz der abstrakten Monumentalität zu gestalten. Mit dem Innenraum schuf er als subtiles kulminierendes Ereignis das, was wir inzwischen einen «Raum der Intellektion» nennen – das «Offene» –, eine fast direkte Manifestation des Wortes des Philosophen.

Pao-Chi Chang studierte Architektur an der St. John's University, Shanghai und am Illinois Institute of Technology, wo Mies van der Rohe ihr Diplombetreuer war (Thema: die Chicago Convention Hall). Nachdem sie eine Zeitlang im Büro von Mies tätig war, wechselte sie zum Chicago Office of Skidmore, Owings & Merrill, wo sie als Senior Architectural Designer und Project Architectural Designer für viele verschiedene Gebäudetypen verantwortlich war, von den 17 Stationen der Dan-Ryan-Kennedy-Linie des öffentlichen Verkehrsmittelnetzes in Chicago bis zum Sears Tower. Danach war sie Mitgründerin des Büros Alfred Swenson Pao-Chi Chang Architects. Sie war über 20 Jahre lang als Professorin für Architektur am Illinois Institute of Technology und als Gastprofessorin für Architektur an der Harvard Graduate School of Design tätig. Zahlreiche Vorträge und Publikationen zum Thema Architektur und Architekturkritik gehören ebenfalls zu ihrem Schaffen.

Alfred Swenson studierte Architektur am Illinois Institute of Technology, wo er die akademischen Titel B.A. und M.A. erlangte. Bei C. F. Murphy Associates war er als Architectural Designer an der Gestaltung des Gerichtsgebäudes sowie des Bürogebäudes des Richard J. Daley Centers beteiligt. Danach war er Mitgründer des Büros Alfred Swenson Pao-Chi Chang Architects. Er war über 25 Jahre als Professor für Architektur am Illinois Institute of Technology und als Gastprofessor für Architektur an der Harvard Graduate School of Design tätig. Zahlreiche Vorträge und Publikationen zum Thema Architektur und Architekturkritik gehören ebenfalls zu seinem Werk.

Crown Hall des IIT in Chicago, 1950–56

Die Crown Hall ist das Gebäude für Architektur, Stadt- und Regionalplanung auf dem Campus des Illinois Institute of Technology. Das Stahl- und Glasgebäude ist ohne innere Stützen. Das Dach ist an vier Stahlträgern aufgehängt. In der Halle, einem ganz großen Raum mit niedrigen Wandabschlüssen, sind Zeichenraum, Bibliothek und Ausstellungsraum untergebracht. Im Untergeschoß befinden sich die Werkstätten, Unterrichtsräume, Kleiderablagen und Waschgelegenheiten.

Crown Hall ist eine große Halle, die nur durch niedere Trennwände gegliedert ist und in welcher Hunderte von Studenten arbeiten. Sie wirkt befreiend, da ihre Einzelräume nicht einengen, aber auch nicht zu anderen Räumen in Beziehung stehen; stets ist aber der ganze Mechanismus des Gebäudes und des Betriebs sichtbar und spürbar. Eine eingehängte Decke löst die Probleme der Akustik und der Beleuchtung. Die Verglasung ist fest und die Klimatisierung dadurch möglich; für das Arbeiten in einer klimatisch ungünstigen und schmutzigen Großstadt ist diese Konzeption richtig. Die Halle ist wechselnden Zwecken anzupassen; Tagungen und große Ausstellungen können abgehalten werden; aber es wäre auch eine radikale Veränderung der Funktion denkbar.

Sein Suchen nach einer klaren Struktur führt Mies van der Rohe einerseits zur Vervollkommnung des Skeletts, andererseits zu immer größeren, freieren Innenräumen. Wir erkennen in diesem Projekt deutlich das Denken eines Ingenieurs; er hängt die äußere Glashülle an einer großen Binderkonstruktion auf und stülpt das ganze Gebäude einem Inhalt über, der erst in einem zweiten Arbeitsgang vollendet werden muß.

Seit Mies van der Rohe 1939 den Auftrag für den Neubau des Illinois Institute of Technology erhielt, beschäftigte ihn diese Aufgabe vordringlich. Heute ist etwa die Hälfte der Institutsbauten fertig erstellt. Der über das ganze Gebiet gelegte Raster hat eine Seitenlänge von 24 Fuß, also etwa 8 Metern. Mies sagte: «Das Illinois Institute of Technology war die größte Entscheidung, die ich je zu

Crown Hall at IIT in Chicago, 1950–56

Crown Hall is the building for architecture and urban and regional planning on the campus of the Illinois Institute of Technology. The steel and glass building has no interior supports. The roof is suspended from four steel girders. The drawing room, library and exhibition room are located in the main hall, a very large space with low partitioning walls. The workshops, classrooms, wardrobes and lavatories are on the basement level.

Crown Hall is a large hall structured by low partitioning walls; hundreds of students at a time can be found working within this space. It has a liberating effect since the individual rooms within the hall are not restrictive and are not placed in relation with each other; but the entire mechanism of the building and the operations is always visible and present. The glazing is fixed in place; air conditioning is therefore practicable. This conception is appropriate for working in a climatically unfavorable and dirty city. The hall is adaptable to a variety of functions and purposes that change all the time; conferences and large exhibitions can be held within, but a radical alteration of its function is also conceivable.

Mies van der Rohe's search for a clear structure, on the one hand, led him to perfect the skeletal structure and, on the other, to create increasingly large, wide open interiors. In this project, we clearly recognize his engineer's thinking and methodology; he suspends the outer glass shell from a large binding construction and places the entire building on top of a substance that needed to be completed only in a second work phase.

Mies van der Rohe was predominantly occupied with the construction of the Illinois Institute of Technology after receiving the commission in 1939. Today, about half of the institutional buildings have been completed. The grid stretches across the entire area and has a lateral length of 24 feet, or about 8 meters. "The Illinois Institute of Technology was the biggest decision I ever had to make. We began construction over fifteen years

treffen hatte. Vor mehr als fünfzehn Jahren haben wir mit Bauen begonnen, und bis heute hätte alles fertig sein sollen – aber natürlich wird es noch einmal zehn Jahre dauern. Einen einzelnen Bau kann man, wenn er einmal gebaut ist, stehenlassen und weggehen. Aber 25 Jahre sind heutzutage eine lange Zeit – und ich wußte, daß unsere Bauweise diese Spanne überdauern müßte, ohne überholt zu sein. Architektur gilt nicht nur für den Augenblick, sondern für die Epoche. Diese Bauten werden nicht altern ... sie wurden verwirklicht, so wie man sie heute verwirklichen sollte: indem man unsere technischen Möglichkeiten ausnützte. Sie sollten einfach sein; und sie sind einfach. Aber nicht primitiv einfach, sondern edel, ja monumental.»

ago, and everything was supposed to be completed by today – but, of course, it will take at least another ten years. Once it is built, you can simply leave an individual building alone and walk away. But 25 years is a long time these days – and I knew that our construction style would have to endure over time without becoming outdated. Architecture does not apply only to the moment but for the entire epoch. These buildings won't age ... they were realized as they would be realized today: by exploring our technical possibilities. They should be simple, and they are simple. Not simple in a primitive way but instead in a noble, even monumental way," said Mies van der Rohe.

Die Grundlage

Die Crown Hall auf dem Campus des IIT mit distributiven Zellen unter einem gemeinsamen Dach ist innen frei von Stützen. Der Innenraum hat eine Ausdehnung von 36 x 66 m. Das Dach ist an der Unterseite an vier Stahl-Fachwerkbindern aufgehängt, die ihrerseits von je vier außenstehenden Stahlstützen getragen werden. Diese Stützen stehen im Abstand von 18 m, und das Dach kragt an jedem Ende 6 m aus. Die gesamte Außenwand besteht aus festen Glasscheiben zwischen Stahlpfosten, die mit der äußeren Stahlverkleidung der Fußboden- und der Deckenplatte verschweißt sind. Die unteren Scheiben der ausfachenden Außenwände sind sandstrahl-mattierte Glastafeln, die oberen Füllungen Klarglas mit Innenjalousien.

Bei der Crown Hall wird die architektonische Idee von Mies zur überzeugenden Wahrheit. Die Struktur erreicht eine makellose Schönheit. «Ich glaube, daß dies der klarste Bau ist, den wir je schufen, und der beste, was den Ausdruck unserer Philosophie betrifft.»

The Basis

Crown Hall on the campus of IIT, with disbursed cells beneath a common roof, has no interior supports. The interior volume spans 36 x 66 meters. The roof is suspended from the bottom of four steel girders; the girders are each supported by four steel supports on the exterior. These supports are placed at a distance of 18 meters; the roof cantilevers 6 meters on each end. The entire outer wall consists of fixed glass panels stretched between the steel supports, which are welded together with the outer steel encasing of the floor and ceiling panels. The lower panels of the outer walls consist of sandblasted matt glass panels; the upper fillings are clear glass with Venetian blinds on the inside.

Crown Hall makes the architectural idea of Mies a convincing truth. The structure achieves a flawless beauty. "I believe that this is the clearest building we have ever created and the best when it comes to the expression of our philosophy."

Zur Situation

Der nach Süden orientierte terrassenartige Haupteingang der Crown Hall erwies sich für die Studenten als zu weit weg vom Campuszentrum liegend, so daß der kleinere Nebeneingang benützt wurde. Es stört aber bei diesem allseitigen Glasvolumen absolut nicht, die dem Campus zugewandte Rückseite zu benützen.

Der Campus des Illinois Institute of Technology (IIT) von 1939–56 ist aufgeteilt nach einem Raster von 12 auf 24 Fuß, der alle Elemente der Überbauung bestimmt. Und es gehört zu seiner besonderen Konsequenz, daß Mies van der Rohe an diesem äußeren Anspruch bei den Campusbauten über Jahrzehnte mit nur kleinen Abweichungen festhalten konnte.

About the Location

The terrace-like main entrance of Crown Hall, which is oriented towards the south, proved to be too far away from the center of the campus for the students; therefore, the smaller rear entrance was used. However, this all-round glazed volume is not disturbed by the fact that the rear entrance, which is turned towards the campus, is used.

The campus of Illinois Institute of Technology (IIT) from 1939–56 is divided up into a grid of 12 by 24 feet, dimensions that determine all of the elements of the development. And it is due, in part, to this special consistency that Mies van der Rohe was able to maintain this outer standard for the campus buildings over decades with only slight digressions.

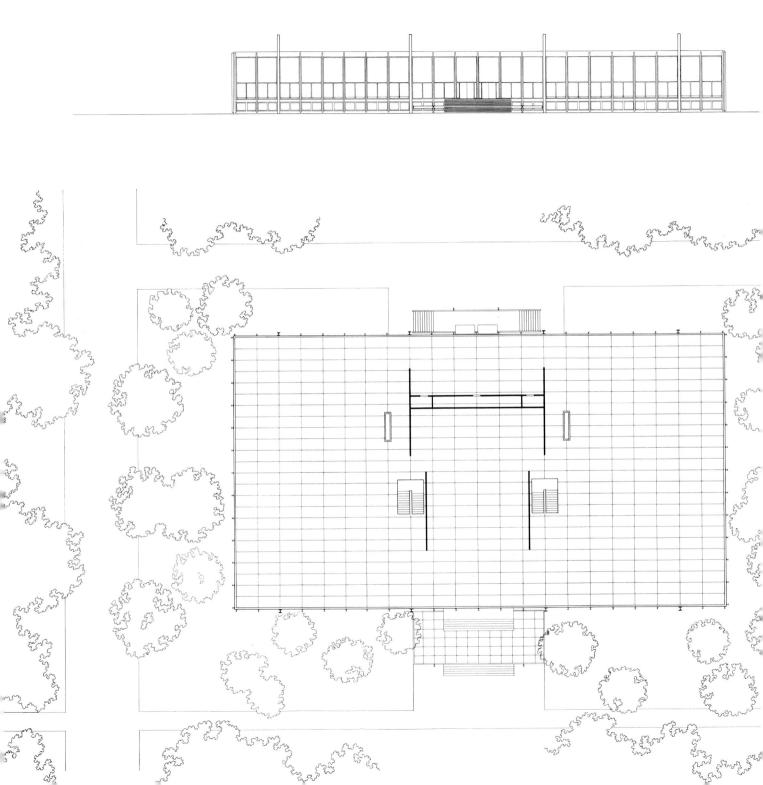

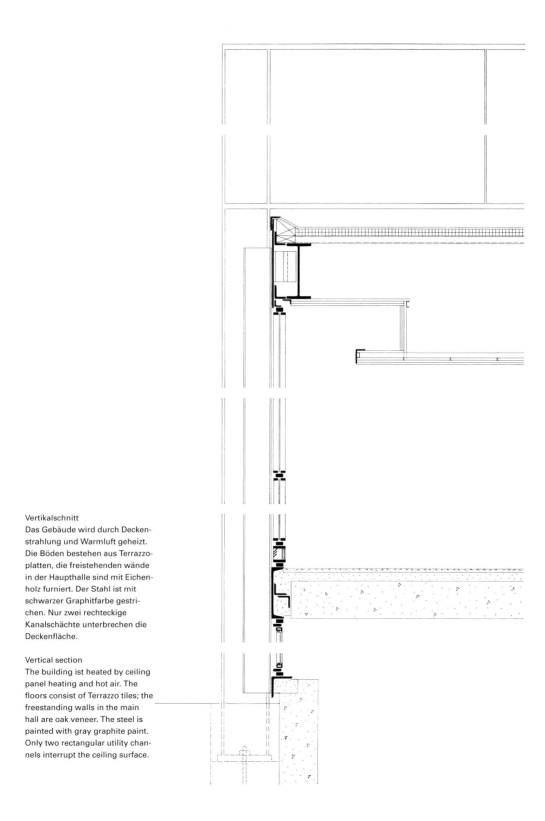

Ansicht und Situation
Nach Mies hat Bauen weniger zu tun mit der Erfindung von Formen als mit der baulichen Gestaltung klarer Sachverhalte.

Elevation and situation
After Mies, building has less to do with the invention of forms than with the architectural design of clear situations and facts.

Vertikalschnitt
Das Gebäude wird durch Deckenstrahlung und Warmluft geheizt. Die Böden bestehen aus Terrazzoplatten, die freistehenden Wände in der Haupthalle sind mit Eichenholz furniert. Der Stahl ist mit schwarzer Graphitfarbe gestrichen. Nur zwei rechteckige Kanalschächte unterbrechen die Deckenfläche.

Vertical section
The building ist heated by ceiling panel heating and hot air. The floors consist of Terrazzo tiles; the freestanding walls in the main hall are oak veneer. The steel is painted with gray graphite paint. Only two rectangular utility channels interrupt the ceiling surface.

Das Rastermaß

Die Halle ist 5,40 m hoch und steht 1,80 m über dem Straßenniveau. Fensterpfosten sind im Abstand von 3 m gesetzt. Die Halle wird durch 3 Gruppen von 1,80 m hohen, freistehenden Wänden in zwei allgemeine Arbeitsräume aufgeteilt, die durch eine große zentrale Ausstellungshalle getrennt sind.

Das Gebäude wird durch Deckenstrahlung und Warmluft geheizt. Die Böden bestehen aus Terrazzoplatten, die freistehenden Wände in der Haupthalle sind mit Eichenholz furniert. Der Stahl ist mit schwarzer Graphitfarbe gestrichen. Nur zwei rechteckige Kanalschächte unterbrechen die Deckenfläche.

In bezug auf die Crown Hall, einem seiner letzten Gebäude, sagte Mies, daß er das normale Rastermaß verlassen habe. «Ich verwendete das Raster einfach in einem größeren Maßstab. Die einzelnen Teile fügen sich damit nicht mehr in das Rastermaß, das bei den normalen Hochschulgebäuden 24 Fuß mißt, während hier der Stützenabstand 60 mal 120 Fuß groß ist. Ich glaube, die Crown Hall ist das vollkommenste, das durchdachteste und das einfachste Bauwerk. Die anderen Gebäude gehorchen einer mehr sachlichen Ordnung auf einer vorwiegend wirtschaftlichen und nützlichen Ebene, das Architekturgebäude dagegen mehr einer geistigen Ordnung.»

The Grid Dimensions

The hall is 5.40 m high and stands 1.80 m above ground level. Window posts are placed at a distance of 3 m. The hall is divided into two general work areas by 3 groups of free-standing walls with a height of 1.80 m; these two areas are separated by a large central exhibition hall.

The building is heated by ceiling panel heating and forced hot air. The floors consist of Terrazzo tiles; the freestanding walls in the main hall are oak veneer. The steel is painted with black graphite paint. Only two rectangular utility channels interrupt the ceiling surface.

Mies van der Rohe said that he had deviated from the standard grid dimensions in Crown Hall, one of his last buildings. "I simply applied the grid in a larger scale. Thus the individual elements are no longer integrated into the grid size, which is 24 feet in the other buildings. Here, the distance between the supports is 60 feet and the span is 120 feet. I believe Crown Hall is the most perfected building, the best conceived and the simplest. The other buildings conform to a more factual order on a mainly economic and practical level; the building for architecture, however, conforms rather to a spiritual order."

Die Außenhülle

Die erhöhte Plattform von 1,80 m über dem Erdboden schafft eine klare Ebene für die Konstruktion und verstärkt den Gedanken der von außen sichtbaren, vortretenden Säulen im T-Profil bei der Aufhängung des Dachbinders. In diesem vertikalen und horizontalen Konstruktionsprinzip liegt ein weit sichtbares Signal der Erneuerung und zugleich ein unübersehbarer Akzent, der das Gebäude visuell und faktisch erschließt.

Mies van der Rohes Philosophie war es, daß im Bauwerk die Funktion, nicht aber die Gestalt wechselt. Mit stützenfrei überspannten Räumen schuf er die klarsten Varianten seiner Architektur. Der großzügige Einzelraum für 300–400 Studierende drückt die Einheit und die Prinzipien des Lehrplanes aus.

Das 36 x 66 m messende Dach des anderthalbgeschossigen Gebäudes der Crown Hall wird von vier Rahmen getragen und ist an vier Vollwandbindern aufgehängt. Damit wurde die Idee der großen Freifläche realisiert, und es wurden die nötigen Funktionsbereiche für die Studenten und ihre Aktivitäten geschaffen – ohne auf eine ausgewogene Ästhetik zu verzichten. Ein altgriechischer Satz von Perikles drückt diese Gesinnung treffend aus: «Wir lieben das Schöne und bleiben schlicht, wir philosophieren und werden nicht müßig.»

The Outer Shell

The raised platform, which stands 1.80 meters above ground level, creates a clear plane for the construction and emphasizes the idea of the projecting T-profile columns, which are visible from the outside at the suspension points of the roof girders. In this vertical and horizontal construction principle lies a symbol of renewal that is visible from afar, and, at the same time, an unmistakable accentuation that visually and factually develops the building.

Mies van der Rohe's philosophy was that the function in a building could change, but not the design. With support-free, spanned spaces he created the clearest versions of his architecture. The generous single space for 300-400 students expresses the unity and principles of the curriculum.

The roof of the one and a half story building of Crown Hall has a dimension of 36 x 66 meters; it is supported by four frames and suspended from four plain web girders. This fulfilled the idea of the large open space and created the necessary functional sections for the students and their activities without giving up on a balanced aesthetic. An old Greek maxim coined by Pericles expresses this philosophy to the point: "We love beauty and remain simple, we philosophize and don't become idle."

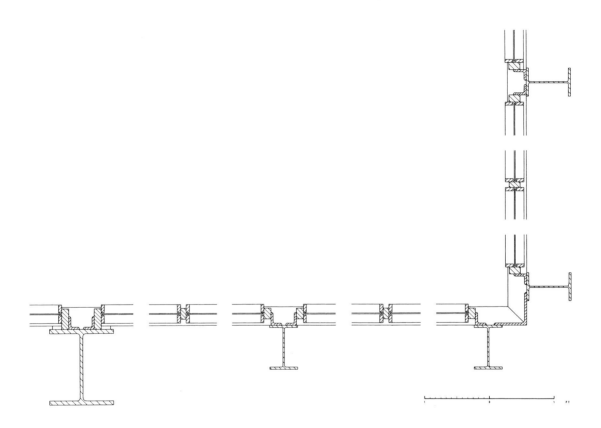

Horizontalschnitt

Horizontal section

Die stützenfreie Halle

Die Crown-Hall am IIT ist eine Schulung und Bildung integrierende Halle. Der Grossraum als leerer Raum ist in ständiger Bewegung. Da, wo Teams und Semesterklassen sich einer gegebenen Aufgabe stellen, wird der Arbeitsplatz jeweils ideenreich eingerichtet. Vielleicht wird in der allseits verglasten Halle manchmal eine Klausur nötig, um in den vielschichtigen Funktionen von Schulung, Ausstellung und Forum Konzentration zu finden. Insgesamt ist es eine beeindruckende Bestätigung dafür, wie wenig Mittel räumliche Veränderungen brauchen, und wie dadurch architektonische Kreativität kontinuierlich zur Entfaltung kommt.
Und es ist ein Ort, wo sich der Student heimisch fühlt, wo ihn die ausgeklügelt ruhige Ästhetik zurückruft auf das Wesenhafte in der Architektur und wo er das Maß seiner eigenen Inspiration finden kann. Die freitragende Spannweite großer Maßstäbe setzt nicht nur konstruktives Verständnis voraus, sondern auch die Fähigkeit, ihre innere Ordnung zu erleben. Im universalen Unterrichtsraum der Crown Hall beeinflusst der vollkommene Raum das Schaffen von Lernenden und Lehrern.

The Hall Without Interior Support

Crown-Hall at IIT is a hall that combines technical education and practical training. The large space, an empty void, is in a constant state of flux. Where teams of students and curriculum courses deal with given tasks, the workspace is set up in ever-new and inventive ways. Perhaps at times a private sanctuary becomes necessary within the all-round glazed hall in order to find concentration in the midst of all the multi-layered functions of education, exhibitions and forums. Altogether, it is an impressive confirmation for how few means are required for spatial changes and how, as a result, architectural creativity is continuously unfolding. And it is a place where students can feel at home, where the sophisticatedly calm aesthetics call them back to the essential in architecture and where they can find the extent of their own inspiration. The spanning of space on a large scale without interior support not only presumes a constructive understanding but also the ability to experience an inner order. In the universal classroom of Crown Hall, the perfected space influences the creativity of both students and teachers.

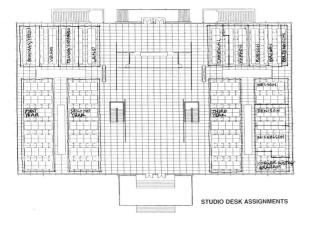

Crown Hall: Raumbelegung für Architektur-Semester und Studios, Januar 1999.

Crown Hall: usage plan for architectural semesters and studios, January 1999.

Der Innenraum

Der leere Raum im Obergeschoß von 5,40 m Höhe, in dem die verschiedenen Semester der Architekturabteilung geschult werden, steht in Kontrast zum Untergeschoß, dem früheren Institute of Design, heute die Modellwerkstatt mit Vorlesungssaal der Studenten. Daraus ergibt sich die programmatische Absicht, einen phantastischen Großraum, gleichsam eine «jewel box», herzustellen. Feingliedrige Lamellen, die den Lichteinfall dosieren, schließen die Box allseits nach außen ab.

Die Entwicklung dieser architektonischen Gestalt hat Mies van der Rohe zu jenem extremen Punkt getrieben, wo sich physische Formen mit geistigem Inhalt verbinden. Der weite Innenraum ist säulenfrei mit der Tragstruktur überspannt, von kleinteiligen Einbauten befreit und kann je nach Bedarf – neben der klaren Funktionalität als Ausbildungsraum – auch für Ausstellungen genutzt werden.

Mit seinem Raumkonzept der Leere tendierte Mies van der Rohe dazu, mit gestalterischer Geschlossenheit und kühler Eleganz Ruhe zu schaffen. Der Baukörper wurde so optimiert, daß der stützenfreie Innenraum mit einem hohen Atrium zu vergleichen ist. Das Innen ist zum permanenten Wechsel bereit, den Benutzern wird im Gebrauch keine Ästhetik aufgedrängt, sie sind aber nachhaltig aufgerufen, mit der Leere zur Lehre zu finden.

The Interior

With a height of 5.40 meters, the open space on the upper floor, where the students of the architectural department, from first-year to graduates, are trained, stands in contrast to the basement floor, the former Institute of Design and today the modeling workshop with a lecture hall. What results is the programmatic intention to create a fantastic large space and at the same time a "jewel box." Filigree lamellas on all sides, which regulate the entering light, close off the box towards the outside.

The development of this architectural design was driven by Mies van der Rohe to that extreme point where physical forms merge with spiritual content. The vast interior has no columns and is spanned by the supporting structure. It is free of small, superfluous installations and, aside from its clear function as an educational space and depending on the requirements, it can also be used for exhibitions.

With his spatial concept of emptiness Mies van der Rohe tended towards creating peace and calm via the completeness of the design, and a cool elegance. The building volume was optimized in a way such that the support-free interior can be compared with a high atrium. The interior is ready for frequent changes. No artificial aesthetic sensibility is forced upon the users, but they are effectively called upon to find instruction through emptiness.

Mies van der Rohe – Chicago-Schule 1938–56

Die Voraussetzung
Die Technik soll Vertrautheit geben. Wir sollen lernen, mit ihr aus dem Material der Gegenwart zu arbeiten. Sie ist die materielle Grundlage unseres Bauens. Denn wir sind eine Generation des technischen Zeitalters. Chicago ist völlig aus dem Geiste dieses technischen Zeitalters erbaut. Die Stahlindustrie bestimmt von vornherein das architektonische Gesicht Chicagos. In den achtziger Jahren hat der Architekt Louis Sullivan die «Chicago-Schule» begründet. Es entstanden die ersten Wolkenkratzer der Welt aus einem Rahmenwerk von Stahlskeletten. Ein bezeichnender Begriff der Arbeitsweise Mies van der Rohes ist «skin and skeleton». Mit diesem Begriff wird eine Arbeitsweise umschrieben, indem streng zwischen rein konstruktiven und bloß verkleidenden Bauelementen unterschieden wird. So wurde es möglich, die konventionellen Bauweisen von Stein- und Holzbau durch große Öffnungen zu sprengen. Auf dieser rein stofflichen Voraussetzung baut Ludwig Mies van der Rohe sein Programm auf.

Sein Programm
«Das Ziel der fortgeschrittenen Übungen ist es, Klarheit zu gewinnen über die Grundgesetze der Architektur: Konstruktion als Faktor der Architektur; ihre Möglichkeiten und Begrenzungen. – Raum als Architekturproblem. – Proportion als architektonisches Ausdrucksmittel. – Ausdruckswert der Materialien. – Malerei und Plastik in ihrer Beziehung zur Architektur und die Anwendung dieser Prinzipien in freier schöpferischer Arbeit.» Sein Programm ist also die Lösung aller architektonischen Probleme von fundamentalen Prinzipien her. In die elementare Besinnung ist die Umreißung aller Möglichkeiten und aller Grenzen eingeschlossen. Das Wesen des Raumes ist nicht bestimmt durch das bloße Vorhandensein begrenzender Flächen, sondern durch das geistige Prinzip dieser Begrenzung. Die Gestaltung des Raumes bereits von der Struktur her ist die eigentliche Aufgabe der Architektur. Nicht das Gebäude

Mies van der Rohe – Chicago School 1938–56

The Precondition
Technology is to provide us with familiarity. We should learn to work with it from the material of the present. It's the material foundation of our building. Because we're a generation of the technological age. Chicago has been built entirely out of the spirit of this technological age. The steel industry determined the architectural mien of Chicago from the onset. During the eighties, the architect Louis Sullivan founded the "Chicago School." The first high-rise buildings of the world using steel skeleton frames were created. A characteristic term of the working method of Mies van der Rohe is "skin and skeleton." This term describes a way of working by strictly distinguishing between the purely constructive and the encasing building elements. It thus became possible to go far beyond the scope of the conventional construction methods of stone and wood. Ludwig Mies van der Rohe established his program based on this purely material precondition.

His Program
"The object of the advanced work is the clarification of: The structure as an architectural factor; its possibilities and limitations. – Space as a means of architectural expression. – Proportion as a means of architecture. – The expression value of materials. – Painting and sculpture in their relationship to architecture and the application of these principles by means of free creative work." Hence, through fundamental principles, his program is the solution of all architectural problems. The embracing of all possibilities and limitations is included in the elementary consciousness. The essence of the space is not determined by the pure existence of limiting surfaces but by the spiritual principle of this limitation. The design of the space in its structure is the true task of architecture. It is not the building that is the work of art but the space. All art is based on a law of proportions as a symbol of the organizing power of man. The shapeless matter receives a shape through pro-

Aus dem Verzeichnis der «Meisterkurse 1944/45» des Illinois Institute of Technology, Chicago; Architekturabteilung Prof. Mies van der Rohe, Prof. Hilbersheimer, Prof. Peterhans.

From the curriculum of the "Master Courses 1944/45" of the Illinois Institute of Technology, Chicago; Dept. of Architecture Prof. Mies van der Rohe, Prof. Hilbersheimer, Prof. Peterhans.

ist das Kunstwerk, sondern der Raum. Aller Kunst liegt ein Gesetz der Proportionen zugrunde, als Zeichen der ordnenden Kraft des Menschen. In der Proportion bekommt die gestaltlose Materie Gestalt: Zeugnis der Herrschaft des menschlichen Geistes. Die Proportion muß darum das entscheidende Mittel der architektonischen Expression sein. Aber keine Form ohne Bezug zum Material. Der Ausdruckswert des Materials steht nicht hinter dem der Form zurück. Es ergibt sich die Notwendigkeit, die materialgerechte Form oder das formgerechte Material zu finden. Die künstlerische Aussage ist eine Aussage der Einheit von Gestalt und Stoff. Daraus ergibt sich wiederum die Notwendigkeit, Kunstwerke des Pinsels oder des Meißels in die Raumgestaltung von vornherein schöpferisch miteinzubeziehen. In den großen Epochen der Kulturgeschichte war dies – den Baumeistern eine wohl nicht bewußte – Selbstverständlichkeit. Unsere Generation ist gezwungen, sich der geistig-künstlerischen Einheit wieder bewußt zu werden. Der Geist ist eine Einheit, und diese Einheit muß wieder gesucht werden.

Wie sich im Einzelleben die Person, so muß sich im kulturellen Gesamtleben die geistige Einheit, die Gestalt, integrieren. Es bleibt das Verdienst von Ludwig Mies van der Rohe, der Architektur den Weg in die Tiefe des Geistes und damit in seine Einheit wieder gewiesen zu haben. Wir, seine Schüler, haben die Aufgabe, die geistige Beschaffenheit der architektonischen Probleme zu erkennen und in schöpferischer Freiheit zu lösen. Nicht das Was, sondern das Wie sollte Ludwig Mies van der Rohe uns zeigen. Seine Realisationen in Chicago 1938–1956 setzen die Tradition der «Chicago-Schule» fort.

(Aus: Bauen und Wohnen, WB, 1956)

portion: bearing witness to the power of the human spirit. The proportion therefore has to be the decisive tool in architectural expression. But there's no form without a relationship to the material. The expressive power of the material does not stand behind that of the form. What results is the necessity of finding the form that is appropriate to the material, or the material appropriate to the form. The artistic expression is an expression of the unity of form and material. From this results the necessity to integrate works of art of a brush or chisel into the spatial design from the onset in a creative way. During the great epochs of cultural history this was self-understood, although probably not at a conscious level with respect to the building masters. Our generation is compelled to once again create the spiritual-artistic unity in a conscious way. The spirit is a unity, and this unity has to be searched again.

Like the all of us in our individual lives, the spiritual unity, the form, has to be integrated into the overall cultural life. It remains the merit of Ludwig Mies van der Rohe to have shown to architecture the way into the depth of the spirit and thus into its unity. We, his students, have the task to recognize the spiritual essence of the architectural problems and to solve them through creative freedom. Ludwig Mies van der Rohe didn't want to show us the "What" but the "How." His realizations in Chicago 1938-1956 continue the tradition of the "Chicago School."

(from: Bauen und Wohnen, WB, 1956)

Mies – Stufen seiner Entwicklung

Mies van der Rohe, 1886 in Aachen geboren, 1969 in Chicago gestorben, war schon zu Lebzeiten eine legendäre Persönlichkeit. Sein maßstabsetzendes Werk faszinierte von Anfang an.

Eines seiner wegweisenden Bauwerke stellt den gestaltungsgeschichtlich bedeutsamen Entwicklungsschritt zur freistehenden, von der Konstruktion unabhängigen Wand dar: Der Barcelona-Pavillon von 1928/29, seit 1986 wieder aufgebaut, läßt die Idee der eingeschobenen Wand beispielhaft nachvollziehen. Diese ästhetische Aufwertung der Wände nutzte Mies zugleich als Hommage an die edlen Stein-Materialien Onyx und Marmor.

Mies van der Rohe schuf auf dem amerikanischen Kontinent in Distanz zu europäischen Einflüssen seine originären Bauwerke im Skin-and-Skeleton-System, die zu einer unverstellten, neuen Sicht auffordern. Dies im bewußten Rückgriff auf den «offenen» Grundriß, der nun durch eine Neubewertung von Offenheit und Transparenz gekennzeichnet ist. So etwa im Großraum der Crown Hall am IIT (1950–56), in dem die Freude der Benutzer in faszinierender Weise zum Ausdruck kommt. Bau und Leben werden eins.

Mies van der Rohe errichtete in Chicago 1948–51 am Michigansee die 860 Lake Shore Drive Apartments. Diese Gebäude – mit Parallelen zu den Fassaden-Hochhaus-Beispielen der ersten Chicago-Schule – gelten als Gründungshochhäuser der modernen Architektur. Das T-Doppelträger-System in Stahl mit allseitig vollverglasten Geschossen macht die Idee der Moderne umfassend greifbar.

Mies – Steps of his Development

Mies van der Rohe, born 1886 in Aachen/Germany, died in 1969 in Chicago, was a legend of his own time. His work set standards and was fascinating right from the beginning.

One of his trendsetting buildings represents the important developmental step, in terms of design history, toward the free-standing wall independent from the architectural structure: the Barcelona Pavilion from 1928/29, reconstructed in 1986, allows us to understand the idea of an inserted wall in an exemplary way. This aesthetic revaluation of the walls was simultaneously used by Mies as an homage to the noble materials onyx and marble.

Mies van der Rohe created his original buildings using the skin and skeleton system that invite us to take a new, unobstructed view of the American continent while distancing ourselves from European influences. He did so with a conscious referral to the "open" ground plan that is now characterized by a revaluation of openness and transparency. This is the case, for example, in the large space at Crown Hall at IIT (1950–56), where the joy of the users is expressed in a fascinating way. Building and life become one.

Mies van der Rohe built the 860 Lake Shore Drive Apartments on Lake Michigan in Chicago in 1948–51. These buildings – with parallels to the façade high-rise examples of the first Chicago School – are considered foundational high-rise-buildings of modern architecture. The steel I-beam girder system with all-round glazing makes the concept of modernism tangible in a comprehensive way.

Wer im Bauwerk der Konstruktion das Primat zuerkennt, huldigt nicht einem l'art pour l'art. Im vollkommenen Bauwerk beglaubigt sich die Kunst selbst. Mies gelang es, Vorgestelltes ins Faßbare, geistig Entwickeltes ins Wirkliche, Ideelles ins Gestaltgebende zu transferieren. Seine Architektur führt nahezu zum Nichts, denn an der Kunst der Fuge beginnt seine besondere Gestalt. Das Notwendige der einfachen oder raffiniertesten Konstruktion, das Primäre der Struktur übt eine suggestive Wirkung aus. Diese Wirkung betrifft die innerliche künstlerische Wirksamkeit: subtil konstruiert mit differenzierter Transparenz.

Those who assign the primal to construction in a building don't pay homage to a "l'art pour l'art." Art authenticates itself in a perfect building. Mies succeeded in transferring ideas into something tangible, spiritual developments into reality, ideals into the principles of design. His architecture almost leads to nothingness because his special design begins with the art of the joint. What's necessary about a simple or highly sophisticated construction, what's primary in a structure, has a suggestive effect. This effect concerns the inner artistic effectiveness: subtly constructed with a differentiating transparency.

Mies persönlich – zur Lehre

Mies van der Rohe hat sich schon während seiner europäischen Periode, so etwa am Bauhaus in Dessau und Berlin 1930–33, mit der praktischen Erziehung der Architekten beschäftigt und dies auch in Schriften festgehalten. Im Alumni Memorial Hall-Gebäude am IIT, später in der Crown Hall, fand auch der Unterricht der Architektenausbildung statt. Es war eine Chance für die Studenten, die Verwirklichung der Prinzipien einer Glas- und Stahlarchitektur unmittelbar erleben zu können. Theoriesaal und Bauplatz waren nebeneinander. Mies als Architekt und Lehrer ist mit seiner Schule und dem Unterrichtsraum eng verbunden. Mies hat über zwei Jahrzehnte am IIT gewirkt, nicht nur als dozierender Redner, sondern mehr noch als Meister, der am Zeichentisch die Probleme seinen Studenten aufzeigte und sie mit ihnen löste. Er hat nur wenig Theoretisches niedergeschrieben, da es ihm mehr um die ständige Präzisierung der Aufgabe, als um die nachträgliche Reflexion ging. Alles bei ihm war Praxis, war Arbeit bis ins Detail, streng kritisch.

Prinzipielle Projekte entwickelte Mies mit seinen Schülern am IIT, oft bevor sich eine praktische Gelegenheit zur Ausführung bot. Zu den Voraussetzungen jeder Planung gehörte ein intensives Studium des Baumaterials und seiner Verwendbarkeit. Dies geschah im Kurs unter Anwendung von Collagen. Das konstruktive Gefüge wurde auf seine Möglichkeiten und Grenzen hin analysiert und die Beziehung von Raum und Proportion, also die modulare Koordination, am Modell geprüft. Die Studentenarbeiten erstrecken sich von der kleinen Zelle bis zur riesigen Halle, vom Wohnhaus über das öffentliche Gebäude bis hin zur geplanten Stadt. Die Entwicklung der Fähigkeiten der Studenten erfolgte über visuelles Training (Photomontage und Collagen), am Zeichentisch, in der Werkstatt (Modellstudie) und anhand von Diplomarbeiten (graduate courses).

Mies Personally – About the Teaching

Mies van der Rohe was already dealing with the practical training of architects during the European period – for example, at Bauhaus in Dessau and Berlin 1930–33 – and he wrote down all of his ideas. In the Alumni Memorial Hall building at IIT, and later in Crown Hall, the architectural training classes took place. It was an opportunity for the students to experience the realization of the principles of a glass and steel architecture directly. The theoretical classroom and building site were side by side. Mies, as an architect and teacher, was closely connected with his school and the classroom. He worked at IIT for over two decades not only as a lecturer but also as a master who could show his students problems at the drawing table and solved them together with them. He only wrote down a small amount of theory since his issue was the continuous specification of the task rather than the subsequent reflection. Everything was practice for him, was work down to the details, strictly critical.

Mies developed projects with his students at IIT often before there was a practical opportunity for realization. Among the preconditions of each plan was an intensive study of the building material and its usability. This took place in the course via the application of collages. The constructive structure was analyzed with respect to its possibilities and limitations, and the relationship between space and proportion – the modular coordination – was tested on the model. The students' works ranged from small cell to huge hall, from apartment building to public buildings and planned cities. The development of the skills of the students went from visual training (photomontage and collages) to draftsmanship and workshop skills (model study) to graduate courses.

Büro Mies van der Rohe, Photo 1963
East Ohio Street in Chicago.

Office of Mies van der Rohe, photo 1
East Ohio Street in Chicago.

Porträt Mies in seinem Büro an
der East Ohio Street in Chicago,
1964.

Portrait of Mies in his office at
East Ohio Street in Chicago, 1964.

Biographie		Biography	
1886	Ludwig Mies van der Rohe wird am 27. März in Aachen geboren	1886	Ludwig Mies van der Rohe is born on 27 March in Aachen
1897–1900	Schüler der Domschule in Aachen	1897–1900	Student at Domschule in Aachen
1900–1902	Schüler an der Gewerbeschule der Stadt Aachen, Arbeit im Steinmetzbetrieb seines Vaters	1900–1902	Student at the Gewerbeschule of the city of Aachen, work in the stonemasonry shop of his father
1902	Praktikant auf dem Bau	1902	Practical trainee in construction
1903–1904	Zeichner für Stuckornamente in einem Stuckgeschäft	1903–1904	Draftsman for stucco ornaments in a plaster shop
1905–1907	Möbelzeichner bei Bruno Paul in Berlin	1905–1907	Furniture designer at Bruno Paul in Berlin
1908–1911	Architekt bei Peter Behrens in Berlin, trifft Gropius, Meyer und Le Corbusier	1908–1911	Architect with Peter Behrens in Berlin, meets Gropius, Meyer and Le Corbusier
1912–1937	Eigenes Architekturbüro in Berlin	1912–1937	Architectural office of his own in Berlin
1921–1925	Organisator von Ausstellungen der «Novembergruppe»	1921–1925	Organizer and exhibitions of the "Novembergruppe"
1926	Leiter der Werkbundausstellung «Die Wohnung», Weißenhofsiedlung in Stuttgart	1926	Director of the Werkbund exhibition "Die Wohnung," Weissenhofsiedlung in Stuttgart
1926	Vizepräsident des Deutschen Werkbundes. Wird Mitglied bei den Freunden der «Neuen Russischen Gesellschaft» Denkmal für Karl Liebknecht und Rosa Luxemburg in Berlin (1934 zerstört)	1926	Vice President of Deutscher Werkbund. Becomes a member of the friends of the "Neue Russische Gesellschaft" Memorial for Karl Liebknecht and Rosa Luxemburg in Berlin (destroyed 1934)
1929	Erbauer des Deutschen Pavillons auf der Weltausstellung in Barcelona	1929	Architect of the German pavilion at the World's Fair in Barcelona
1928–1930	Entwurf und Bau der Villa Tugendhat in Brünn	1928–1930	Design and construction of Villa Tugendhat in Brno
1930	Auftrag, die Neue Wache von Schinkel in ein Denkmal für die Gefallenen des Ersten Weltkrieges umzuwandeln	1930	Commission to transform the Neue Wache by Schinkel into a memorial for soldiers killed during World War I
1930–1933	Direktor des Bauhauses in Dessau und Berlin	1930–1933	Director of Bauhaus in Dessau and Berlin
1931	Leiter der Werkbundabteilung «Die Wohnung» an der Berliner Bauausstellung	1931	Director of the Werkbund department "Die Wohnung" at the Berlin architectural tradeshow
1938	Emigration in die USA	1938	Emigration to the United States
1938–1958	Direktor der Architekturabteilung des Illinois Institute of Technology (IIT), Chicago; Neuplanung des Campus	1938–1958	Director of the architectural department at Illinois Institute of

1938	Eigenes Architekturbüro in Chicago			Technology (IIT), Chicago; new plan for the campus
1948	Erste Curtainwalls in Stahl und Glas bei den Wohnhochhäusern in Chicago		1938	Architectural office of his own in Chicago
1950	Entwicklung der stützenlosen Innenräume bei Hallenkonstruktionen mit weitgespannter Dachplatte		1948	First curtain walls in steel and glass in the apartment high-rise buildings in Chicago
1959	Mitglied des Ordens Pour le Mérite (Bundesrepublik Deutschland), Ehrungen und Promotionen in Europa und den USA		1950	Development of the support-free interiors for hall constructions with a broad-span roof
1963	Presidential Medal of Freedom, Ehrung durch den Präsidenten der Vereinigten Staaten		1959	Member of the order Pour le Mérite (Federal Republic of Germany), awards and promotions in Europe and the United States
1969	Ludwig Mies van der Rohe stirbt am 17. August in Chicago		1963	Presidential Medal of Freedom, awarded by the President of the United States
			1969	Ludwig Mies van der Rohe dies in Chicago on 17 August

In kreativer Kraft

Klärende konstruktive Entwicklungen und die Akzeptanz technologischer Möglichkeiten bestimmen die Architekturauffassung von Mies van der Rohe. Seiner Tätigkeit in Chicago galten diese Prinzipien und deren Ausdehnung in die Breite und Tiefe seines Bauvolumens. Bis hin zum großzügigen Zirkulationsraum, in dem sich der Wanderer auf dem IIT-Campus über die Rasenflächen und die weitausragenden Akazienbäume freuen kann. Auf einem Koordinationsnetz mit einem modularen Grundmaß von 24 Fuß, circa 8 Meter, sind die Campusbauten aufgebaut. Die kristalline Wirkung der Baugruppen im Grünen weist auf Frische und Sorgfalt hin, die den Eindruck von Ruhe und Ordnung vermitteln. Gerade hier gilt die gesteigerte Durchdringung von Fülle und Leere, Bauen mit der Natur als Polarität einer intelligenten Zusammenführung.

Es ist darum sinnvoll, wieder an das Werk am IIT zu erinnern, das eine ganze Epoche der «ingeniösen» Architektur geprägt hat. Immer weiter geht das reduktorische Verlangen von Mies dahin, alles auf die konstruktive Genialität und auf die räumliche Einfachheit zurückzuführen. Besonders in seinem Spätwerk korrespondiert die Sparsamkeit der Mittel mit der Sparsamkeit des Ausdrucks. Die Leidenschaft zum Einfachen macht das Vorbild dennoch nicht einfacher. Es braucht das Verstehen der Lehre Mies', um mit der Einfachheit Neues zu entwickeln. Der Bildhauer Constantin Brancusi hat das kühne Wort verbreitet: «Einfachheit ist nicht das Ende, sondern Vollendung.» Und weiter: «Das Schöne ist das absolut Ausgeglichene.»

Ein Großraum für Bildung und Schulung und dennoch Intimität. Die Studenten der verschiedensten Semester sind vermischt, die Ausstellungstafeln auf den eingeschobenen Wänden inspirieren den Lernprozeß. Das Gemeinsame, die Idee der Kooperation wird Wirklichkeit – auch Außenstehende und Gäste sind jederzeit in den Prozeß miteinbezogen. Die Halle in stimulierender Proportion und befreiender Raumhöhe fasziniert die Benutzer und schafft ein geistiges Klima.

In Creative Power

Clarification of constructive developments and the acceptance of technological possibilities determine the architectural conception of Mies van der Rohe. These principles and their penetration into the width and depth of a building volume were applied to his work in Chicago – right up to the generous circulation space, where those wandering through the IIT campus can enjoy the lawns and large acacia trees. The campus buildings are constructed based on a coordination network with a basic modular grid dimension of 24 feet or approximately 8 meters. The crystalline effect of the groups of buildings amidst nature alludes to freshness and carefulness, which communicate peace and order. The enhanced permeation of fullness and void especially applies here, building in concert with nature, the polarity of intelligent merging.

It therefore makes sense to again remember the work at IIT, which has influenced an entire epoch of "ingenious" architecture. The reductive desire of Mies extends to the point where everything is reduced to constructive ingenuity and spatial simplicity. Especially in his late work, the economy of means corresponds with the economy of expression. The passion for simplicity does not, however, make the exemplar simpler. It takes an understanding of Mies van der Rohe's teachings in order to develop something new out of such simplicity. The sculptor Constantin Brancusi coined the bold phrase: "Simplicity is not the end but perfection." – "The beautiful is the absolutely balanced."

A large space for education and training, and yet it's intimate. The students, from freshmen to seniors, are all together; the exhibition panels on the inserted walls inspire learning. The common, the idea of cooperation, becomes a reality, and outsiders and guests are also always integrated into the process. The hall, with its stimulating proportions and liberating spatial height, fascinates the users and creates a spiritual climate.

30. April 1956: Ansprache anläßlich der Einweihungsfeierlichkeiten für die Crown Hall

Dr. Rettaliata!
Als Architekt des Gebäudes bin ich gebeten worden, Ihnen den Schlüssel zu überreichen, wie dies bei einer Einweihung häufig geschieht.
Nachdem ich so lange schon hier gearbeitet habe, konnte ich es mir nicht anders denken, als daß Sie, als der Präsident des Institutes, einen Hauptschlüssel für alle Gebäude des Hochschulgeländes besitzen müssen. So wäre es zwar eine nette, aber im Grunde doch wohl leere Geste, Ihnen einen zweiten Schlüssel zu übergeben.
In früheren Zeiten war das anders.
Man nahm eine derartige Zeremonie durchaus ernst. Sie war nicht so sehr eine Formalität als ein symbolischer Akt.
Ich glaubte, diese alte und weise Tradition wiederaufnehmen zu sollen.
Aus diesem Grunde habe ich einen goldenen Schlüssel für das Gebäude bestellt.
Lassen Sie den Glanz des Goldes ein Symbol sein unserer hohen Wertschätzung Ihrer großen persönlichen Anstrengungen für das Zustandekommen dieses Gebäudes.
Aber Gold glänzt nicht nur.
Es hat noch andere, weniger augenfällige Eigenschaften.
Ich denke an seine Reinheit, seine Beständigkeit – Eigenschaften, die sehr wohl die Art der Arbeit symbolisieren können, die wir in diesem Gebäude zu vollbringen hoffen.
Wir wünschen, daß dieses Gebäude die Heimstätte von Ideen und Abenteuern sein möge.
Realen Ideen.
Ideen, die auf Vernunft beruhen.
Ideen über Tatsachen.
Dann wird das Gebäude für unsere Studenten von großem Nutzen und letzten Endes ein echter Beitrag für unsere Kultur.
Wir wissen, daß das nicht leicht sein wird.
Hohe Dinge sind niemals leicht.
Die Erfahrung lehrt uns, daß sie so schwer sind, wie sie selten sind.

April, 30, 1956: Address at the Dedication of Crown Hall

Dr. Rettaliata,
As the architect of the building I have been asked to present to you the key of the building as it is often done at a dedication.
Working here for so long, I could not help thinking that you, as the President of this Institute must have a master key for all the buildings of the campus. So to give you a second key would be a nice but somewhat empty gesture.
In the days of old it was different. People took a ceremony like this quite seriously. It was not so much a formality as a symbolic act.
I thought I should take up this old and wise tradition. For this reason I ordered a golden key of the building.
Let the brightness of the gold be a symbol of our high appreciation for your great personal efforts to make this building a reality.
But gold is not only bright.
It has other more hidden qualities.
I am thinking of its purity and its durability.
Properties which very well could symbolize the character of the work which we hope will be performed in this building.
Let this building be the home of ideas and adventures.
Real ideas.
Ideas based on reason.
Ideas about facts.
Then the building will be of great service to our students and in the end a real contribution to our civilisation.
We know that will not be easy.
Noble things are never easy.
Experience teaches us that they are as difficult as they are rare.

Ludwig Mies van der Rohe.
Original English manuscript, 1956 University Archives,
Paul V. Galvin Library, Illinois Institute of Technology, Chicago.

Nachwort

Das hohe Qualitätsniveau der Bauten von Mies van der Rohe stimmt optimistisch. Wachheit, offene Augen, inneres Verständnis und auch Kritik sind gefragt. Es gehört zum Konzept der vorliegenden Solitärbauten-Serie, daß auch die direkten Bewohner oder Benutzer zu Worte kommen. Das Spektakuläre ebenso wie das Alltägliche und das leicht zu Übersehende werden in einer individuellen Dimension von den Benutzern auf Brauchbarkeit hin dargestellt. Eine Berichterstattung aus erster Hand also, von Menschen, die das jeweilige Gebäude gleichsam von seinem «Innenleben» her kennen. Bei den vorangegangenen Bänden waren Lord Peter Palumbo für das Farnsworth House und Professor Masami Takayama für die 860 Lake Shore Drive Apartments zuständig. Die beiden Architektur-Professoren, das Ehepaar Pao-Chi Chang und Alfred Swenson, sind als Schüler von Mies geradezu prädestiniert, ihre aktive Erfahrung mit der Crown Hall niederzuschreiben. Für ihren Beitrag gehört ihnen mein aufrichtiger Dank. Einen entsprechenden Essay wird Masami Takayama für den geplanten Band zum IIT-Campus verfassen.

Epilog

The high level of quality of Mies van der Rohe's buildings inspires optimism. Mindfulness of the present, wide-open eyes, an inner understanding and criticism are required. Part of the concept of the present series of solitary buildings is that the inhabitants or users have a direct say. The spectacular and the every-day aspects as well as those aspects that are easily overlooked are presented via an individual range of users with respect to usability; first hand reports from people who know the building in question from its "inner life." In the preceding buildings, Lord Peter Palumbo was in charge of Farnsworth House and Professor Masami Takayama for the 860 Lake Shore Drive apartments. The two architectural professors, the married couple Pao-Chi Chang and Alfred Swenson, are almost predestined as students of Mies to record their active experience with Crown Hall. My sincere gratitude goes to them for their contribution. Masami Takayami will be writing an appropriate essay for the planned volume on the IIT Campus.

Der Basler Architekt und Autor Werner Blaser begann schon in den fünfziger Jahren, die Bekanntschaft mit großen Meistern zu pflegen. Zuerst in Helsinki als Praktikant bei Alvar Aalto, dann in der wichtigen Begegnung mit Mies van der Rohe am Illinois Institute of Technology in Chicago. Blasers Beschäftigung mit der Tradition der Moderne half ihm beim intensiven Studium der klassischen Architektur Japans in Kyoto. In einer editorischen Notiz zu «Fügen und Verbinden» schrieb Charles von Büren: «Der mit seinen 25 Jahren noch wenig erfahrene, aber lern- und wißbegierige Student und Designer Werner Blaser entwickelte sein Sehen und Denken in jenen entscheidenden Jahren im Umkreis von Mies van der Rohe zur bis heute wirksam gebliebenen Form.» Blaser gehört zu jenen Persönlichkeiten, die als humanistische Bau-Meister die Architektur als dienende Kunst im Praktischen und im Schönen konsequent zu Ende denken. Dies findet Ausdruck auch in seinen vielen Publikationen über die Meisterarchitekten des 20. Jahrhunderts sowie in der Serie über elementare Bauten in Holz, Stein oder Metall.

The Basel architect and author Werner Blaser had already begun making the acquaintance of great masters during the fifties. At first as a practical trainee of Alvar Aalto in Helsinki, then with his important encounter with Mies van der Rohe at the Illinois Institute of Technology in Chicago. Blaser's occupation with the tradition of modernism supported him in his intensive studies of classic Japanese architecture in Kyoto. In an editorial for "Joining and Connecting" Charles von Büron wrote, "The student and designer Werner Blaser, who at the age of 25 had little experience but was keen to learn and to expand his knowledge, developed his way of seeing and thinking during those decisive years amidst the circle of people surrounding Mies van der Rohe right up to their current and still effective form." Blaser is among those personalities who as humanistic building masters consistently think of architecture as a serving art in the practical sense as well as with regard to its aspects of the beautiful. This is also expressed in his many publications about the master architects of the 20th century and in the series about elemental buildings in wood, stone or metal.